My Daily Heart-Blossoms

DAILY MEDITATIONS FOR THE HEART, MIND AND SOUL

Sri Chinmoy

ISBN: 978-1-934972-01-4
Aum Publications
86-10 Parsons Blvd.
Jamaica, NY 11432

Introduction

In this series of 365 spiritual illuminations
—one for each day of the year—Sri Chinmoy
leads the reader to the inner wellspring of light
from which all truth comes.

These aphorisms, poems and reflections have
that familiar ring that resonates in the mind
and heart long after they have been read and
absorbed. They are at once absolutely simple
and supremely profound—wisdom spelling over
into poetry ... and poetry that carries the reader
to new heights of realisation.

A book like this can only come from the pen
of a realised spiritual Master. It is meant to be
read and re-read, and forever treasured in the
aspiring hearts of God-lovers and God-seekers
everywhere.

Contents

January

Aspiration

Aspiration leads man to God-Consciousness.

Aspiration is the inner cry, the mounting flame. Aspiration is at our journey's start and it is also at our journey's close. Ours is not an ordinary, earthly, human journey. Ours is a divine journey; therefore, this journey has neither a beginning nor an end. It is a birthless, deathless journey. This journey has a goal, but it does not stop at any goal, for it has come to realise that today's goal is only the starting point of tomorrow's journey. Once we start consciously and sincerely aspiring, we feel that we are walking along Eternity's road and that we shall eternally walk along this road, receiving and achieving light, more light, abundant light, infinite light. We shall offer this light to aspiring humanity so that this world of ours can become the Kingdom of Heaven.

When God comes into your life,
He brings His Compassion-Chimes
To ring inside
Your aspiration-heart.

JANUARY 2

Aspiration is a glowing fire that secretly and sacredly uplifts our consciousness and finally liberates us.

Aspiration, the inner flame. Unlike other flames, this flame does not burn anything. It purifies, illumines and transforms our life. When purification takes place in our lower nature, we hope to see the Face of God. When illumination dawns in our outer nature, we feel that God is near and dear, that He is all-pervading and all-loving. When our nature, both lower and outer, grows into the transformation-flame, we shall realise the truth that God Himself is the inmost Pilot, brightest Journey and highest Goal.

Aspiration-fire is immediate purification.
It powerfully purifies
The sleeping body,
The strangling vital
And the doubting mind.

No aspiration, no realisation.

Some people are under the impression that desire and aspiration are the same thing. Unfortunately, or fortunately, that is not true. They are two totally different things. Desire wants to bind and devour the world. Aspiration wishes to free and feed the world. Desire is the outgoing energy. Aspiration is the inflowing light. Desire says to man, "Possess everything. You will be happy." Poor man, when he wants to possess just one single thing, he sees that he has already been mercilessly caught and possessed by everything in God's Creation. Aspiration says to man, "Realise only one thing, and that thing is God. You will be happy." Fortunate and blessed man: on his way upward and inward, long before he sees God, he feels sublime peace in his inner life and radiating joy in his outer life. Then he feels that the realisation of the supreme Beyond can no longer remain a far cry.

When I am in my desiring mind,
I offer a very painful prayer to my Lord Supreme.
When I am in my aspiring heart,
My Beloved Supreme blesses me
Not only with a soulful meditation
But also with a fruitful satisfaction.

Aspiration is the endless road that leads eternally towards the ever-transcending Beyond.

Aspiration is our inner urge to transcend both the experience and the realisation already achieved. Aspiration can be developed. It is like crossing a street, one step at a time. Each time we aspire, we perform in the very depths of our consciousness a miracle of welcoming the Beyond. Life has an inner door. Aspiration opens it. Desire closes it. Aspiration opens the door from within. Desire closes it from without. Life has an inner lamp. This inner lamp is called aspiration. And when we keep our aspiration burning, it will, without fail, transmit to God's entire Creation its effulgent glow.

I have starved my desire-thoughts.
Therefore my aspiration-flames
Are climbing up very fast
And are about to touch
The Lotus-Feet of my Beloved Supreme.

What we need is aspiration, the search for the truth, and nothing else. When we have that inner cry for truth, we do not need anything else.

Aspiration is a cry within our heart. A child is within you, shedding tears. He is weeping because he wants to transcend himself. This mounting cry, this climbing cry inside our heart we call aspiration. When we aspire with our heart's tears, we see that God is coming down to us from above. The heart is crying and yearning like a mounting flame burning upward. This flame of the heart wants to go up beyond the mind, so it is always rising. And God is constantly descending with His Grace, like a river flowing downward. It is just like two persons meeting; one is on the first floor and the other is on the third floor. So what happens? We go up to the second floor and God comes down to the second floor. There we meet and fulfil each other. When aspiration and Grace meet together, we come to experience the divine fulfilment of union with God.

No, it is not possible
For any inner cry
To remain unheard.

We feel a desire to have God on our side. But we need the aspiration to throw ourselves on God's side.

If one has desire but no aspiration, that is better than having neither desire nor aspiration. He will have many necessary experiences and eventually he will see that there is no fulfilment in desire. Then he will jump into the sea of aspiration. But if one enters again into the realm of desire after having entered into the world of aspiration, that is a real catastrophe. If one does not aspire, we can say that he is just an ignorant fellow; he does not know that there is something called inner peace, inner bliss, inner light. If someone has not seen the light and he stays in a dark room, God will not blame him because he is not aware that there is a room full of light. But after having had inner experiences, if one wants to go back to the ordinary world, then he will be a victim to frustration and inner destruction.

If you really want
To make your desire-story short,
Then start singing immediately
A long aspiration-song.

A heart without aspiration is, without fail, a totally lost voyager.

Once you enter into the spiritual life, never, never go back to the ordinary life. If you go back to the ordinary life, you will be an object of ridicule in the outer world and an object of distrust in the inner world. People will say, "This fellow has failed; that is why he has given up and come back to us." The divine forces in the cosmos will say, "Oh, he does not care for us. He cares more for the life of ignorance," and they will not try to help you any more. Also, you will always make a conscious or unconscious comparison between the divine life you have left and the life you have returned to. This comparison will always be unfavourable to the ordinary life. Your soul, the divine spark within you, will make you feel that you have given up something most precious. Then frustration will loom large in your ordinary life.

Do not lose your aspiration-heart!
If you lose your aspiration-heart,
Your frustration-mind
Will become larger than the largest.

A life of aspiration is a life of peace. A life of aspiration is a life of bliss.

Before we enter into the aspiration-world, we remain in the desire-world. When we live in the desire-world, greatness is of paramount im-portance to us. Even when we first enter into the aspiration-life, in the beginning the message of greatness at times looms large. But the real message of the aspiration-world is goodness. Desire cries for greatness. Aspiration cries for goodness.

Give your heart aspiration.
This is what your heart needs.
Give your life illumination.
This is what your life deserves.

God can be seen on the strength of our inner cry, which we call aspiration, the mounting flame within us.

There is no other way to know what God does, what God has and what God is than through my life of aspiration. My life of aspiration gives me all the Supreme's secrets. It tells me what God secretly does. It tells me what God secretly has. And it tells me what God secretly is. Only my life of aspiration has all the secrets of God at its disposal.

Before I started my aspiration-life
I was a lonely heart.
But now I am
A smiling and dancing world-heart.

Aspiration means calmness. This calmness finds satisfaction only when it is able to express itself through all-seeing and all-loving detachment.

There is a specific way to accelerate realisation and it is called conscious aspiration. God must come first. There must be no mother, no father, no sister, no brother—nothing else but God, only God. True, we want to see God in humanity, but first we have to see Him face to face. Most of us cry for money, name, fame, material success and prosperity; but we do not cry even for an iota of inner wisdom. If we cry sincerely, devotedly and soulfully for unconditional oneness with our Inner Pilot, then today's man of imperfection will be transformed into tomorrow's God, the perfect Perfection incarnate.

As the mouth of my desire-life
Frightens me,
Even so,
The eyes of my aspiration-heart
Strengthen me.

When we aspire, we go far beyond the domain of the physical mind and sit at the Feet of God the Light.

How do we aspire? Through proper concentration, proper meditation and proper contemplation. Aspiration covers both meditation and prayer. He who is praying feels he has an inner cry to realise God, and he who is meditating also feels the need of bringing God's Consciousness right into his being. The difference between prayer and meditation is this: when I pray, I talk, and God listens; and when I meditate, God talks and I listen. When I pray, God has to listen. But when I meditate, when I make my mind calm and quiet, I hear what God has always been saying to me. So both ways are correct.

To realise God
In His transcendental Heights,
Each seeker must have
A very long-range
Aspiration-programme.

Thirst for the Highest is aspiration.

Each time you aspire, I wish to tell you that your
perfection is increasing. Inside your aspiration, perfection is growing and glowing. Sincere
aspiration means the opening of the perfection-lotus.
A lotus, you know, has many petals. Each time you
aspire most soulfully, one petal of the lotus blooms.
And when one petal blossoms, it means perfection is
increasing in the entire lotus.

Aspiration-efforts
Always supply satisfaction-results.
It may take time, at times,
But the results are unmistakably
Sure.

Aspiration is the mounting flame of our divine wish to raise ourselves to the crest and crowning of Divine Perfection.

When you speak of God's Hour, you have to know that it is the divine moment when God wants you to realise Him and to manifest Him here on earth. How can you harmonise God's Hour and your own aspiration? You will do your part. That is to say, you will play your own role most soulfully. Every day before your meditation, you have to aim at a particular goal, and this particular goal is the highest Height, the transcendental Height that you are trying to reach. You can call it the Golden Shore of the Beyond. When the meditation is over, still you have not reached the Highest. Your intention or your soulful will was to reach the Highest, but still you have not reached it. If you feel sorry, if you feel miserable, then I wish to say that you will never be able to reach your goal.

Every aspiration-day
Begins with new possibilities.
Every aspiration-day
Ends with new achievements.

In aspiration and nowhere else dwells man's salvation.

Feel that there is a specific hour, a golden hour, when you are meant to reach your goal. God's Hour is not at your disposal; it belongs to God. At His sweet Will He will offer it to you, but you have every right to imagine that it is here in today's meditation. When today's meditation is over and God's Hour has not struck, do not feel miserable. Tomorrow again during your meditation you have every right to hope for God's Hour.

> *O my heart of aspiration,*
> *Stay with me.*
> *My soul of delight is coming*
> *To take you and me*
> *To Heaven's Ecstasy-Palace.*

A sleepless aspiration-heart is God's endless Satisfaction-Pride.

God's Hour is like a lotus. It blossoms petal by petal. There is a lotus deep within you, but it blooms only one petal at a time. When all the petals have bloomed, then it is a fully blossomed lotus. Like that, God's Hour is in our aspiration. You cannot separate God's Hour from your own aspiration. When your aspiration reaches the Highest, the acme of Perfection, then automatically the lotus which we call God's Hour blossoms fully.

Today what I have
Is a tiny aspiration-seed.
Tomorrow what I shall have
Is a powerfully developed realisation-blossom.

In order to kindle the flame of your aspiration, try to feel that your life is a life of dedication.

My only request to you is not to try to push or pull. God has asked you to aspire, so you aspire. Then it is up to God to give you divine victory. It is up to Him to fulfil your aspiration. Every day make your resolution: "This is what I am going to achieve." You are not trying to aggrandize or feed your ego. But you have to feel that if you can achieve your goal, if you can reach your destination, then only you will become a conscious instrument of the Supreme.

Let your aspiration-heart
Be enduring.
Your dedication-life will automatically
Be assuring.

Aspiration is the soul's awakening.

Now, we are all instruments of the Supreme; all human beings are instruments of the Supreme. But most of us are unconscious instruments. We do not know that we are instruments; we think that we are the doer. But when we enter into the spiritual life, we come to feel that we are not the doer; somebody else is the doer and that somebody else is the Inner Pilot, the Supreme. Right now, just because you have your own individuality and personality, you have every right to feel that you are praying and you are meditating. Then a day will come when you will feel that it is not you who are praying and meditating; it is somebody else and that is the Supreme in you.

How can you lose
In the battlefield of life
If you are already well-acquainted
With the real in you:
Your heart's aspiration-cry?

In the life of aspiration, two things are of paramount importance: will-power and prayer.

Everything depends on the goals you set. Today you may want God-realisation, but again tomorrow you may feel miserable, thinking that if you realise God, then you will not be able to enjoy the world. Early in the morning you may cry for peace, light and bliss in infinite measure. You tell God that you cannot exist without Him. But in the afternoon you may become a total stranger to your own aspiration. You may feel that if you realise God, then God will not allow you to enjoy teeming imperfections, vital life and all that. At that time, do you really want God or do you want the emotional life? At every moment, aspire, aspire. In your aspiration, God's Hour is bound to strike.

No undivine strength,
No hostile force,
No inconscience-monster
Can slow down the fastest speed
Of our aspiration-dedication-boat
That is arriving at the Golden Shore
Of our Beloved Supreme
At His own choice Hour.

Aspiration, in its simplest definition, is a love-ly flame climbing Heavenward.

In the inner world, we offer our aspiration in return for God-realisation. The flame of our aspiration is kindled by God Himself. The fruit of our realisation, too, we get from God directly. God is the Inspirer in us. God is the Eternal Giver. God is the Eternal Receiver in us. God uses aspiration to take us to Himself. God uses realisation to bring Himself to us. God is sacrifice when we live in the world of aspiration. God is sacrifice when we live in the ream of realisation. But God says that there is no such thing as sacrifice. There is only one thing here on earth and there in Heaven, and that thing is called oneness: the fulfilment in oneness and the fulfilment of oneness.

My aspiration,
Like God's compassion,
Will be eternal, infinite and immortal.

In aspiration and nowhere else dwells man's salvation.

There is always some time between the planting of a seed and the harvest. In the spiritual life, the seed is aspiration and the harvest is realisation. Without aspiration, realisation can never dawn. What is aspiration? Is it something that we already have, or is it something we are going to have? It is both. If we say that we have aspiration, we are right because we do think of God and meditate on God at times. If we say that we do not yet have aspiration but are someday going to have it, we are also right, because our love for God is neither spontaneous nor constant. When we sit at the feet of Eternity we realise that aspiration is bound to be followed by realisation. And after we have made friends with eternal time, we come to understand that realisation was always there, hidden in our aspiration.

It seems that my Lord
Has only one thing to do
Day in and day out:
Amplify my heart's aspiration-cry.

JANUARY 21

Aspiration is surrender, and surrender is man's conscious oneness with God's Will.

We are all living in a world of duality, multiplicity and variety. When we want to elevate our consciousness to the Highest and try to aspire, desire, the thief, robs us. He takes away our psychic aspiration, our pure devotion towards God, our surrendering will which we offer to the Almighty Will. The Christ said, "Except a man be born again, he cannot see the Kingdom of God." What do we learn from this lofty message? We learn that the life of desire has to give way to the life of aspiration. If the life of aspiration does not come to the fore, then a new life can never dawn. The Kingdom of God can be established only when we kindle the flame of aspiration deep within us.

My confusion-mind tells me
That life is nothing
But a dreadful nightmare.
My aspiration-heart tells me
That life can be
A lovely dream.
Why not let me give a chance
To my self-giving heart?

The real transformation of human nature comes not through an austere, ascetic life or a complete withdrawal from the world, but through a gradual and total illumination of life. And for that, one needs aspiration. Aspiration, and aspiration alone is the precursor of this illumination.

If you can come to the state of consciousness where you feel that without God you cannot live even for a few minutes, you will realise God. You will realise God at that moment through the strength of your highest aspiration. Your inmost inner flame has to be kindled, and then you have to cry—cry for God as a child cries for his mother. Only then is God-realisation possible.

Each aspiration-second
Is a fast God-approaching day.
Indeed,
This is a supreme experience
In a seeker's life.

If you do not know which way your life-river should flow, then I ask you to follow your heart's aspiration-boat.

The inner teaching. What do we learn from the inner teaching? Aspiration. Aspiration is the inner flame, the mounting cry within us. Each individual has this burning flame within. But unfortunately most of us do not take the trouble to use the flame of aspiration within us. We are fond of using something else in our day-to-day life: desire. Desire is something that binds us. Aspiration is something that frees us. The message of desire is to possess and be possessed. The message of aspiration is to expand, enlarge and immortalise our earthly existence.

Aspiration gradually ascends.
But if you value your aspiration,
Then needless to say
It swiftly ascends.

Your heart's cry is a real treasure. Do not allow your obscure, unlit, discouraging and damaging vital to make light of it. Your heart's cry flies like an eagle to reach the highest goal of your purest soul.

Frustration and depression can never, never help us. When we cry, it must not be from frustration and depression. We must cry from our inmost hearts, with the intense mounting flame of aspiration. This is the cry that takes us to the Highest. Spiritual people must be optimistic because they must have faith in God's Light. We must try to remain in light and not in night or darkness. If we remain in light, then there can be no sense of failure and no frustration.

An unexpected inner cry
Has turned his life's frustration
Into a most powerful
Aspiration-delight.

The life that does not aspire for God-realisation is not worth even an empty eggshell.

When we aspire we can never say that we are unconscious. When we aspire we do the right thing consciously at every moment. When we don not aspire, that is when we are unconscious. So whenever you are sincerely aspiring, feel that you are conscious. When you are not sincerely aspiring, you are unconscious. When you are unconscious, how will you conquer the undivine forces? So let us always aspire. It is in our aspiration that we can be always conscious. Aspiration and our conscious awareness always go together. When we are consciously aspiring, we cannot be unconsciously cherishing undivine thoughts.

O world, do not bind me,
Do not blind me!
Just let me return
To my heart's aspiration-home.

We have to aspire to reach the Golden All, to see the Golden Shore of the Beyond, the ever-transcending Beyond. This is what we expect from aspiration, the mounting flame within us.

How can you give more value to aspiration? You can give more value to aspiration only by knowing what aspiration can give to you. Always try to see the goal inside. You see a fruit. You know that if you eat the fruit, then only you are satisfied. So try to feel that aspiration is a fruit, but it will give you satisfaction only if you eat it. You have to aspire every day, every day. Then, the result you get is realisation.

Aspiration is
A consciously widening opportunity
For golden possibilities.

Aspiration is our inner urge to transcend both the experience and the realisation already achieved.

You will be able to give all value to aspiration when you know that aspiration will give you realisation, aspiration will give you supreme satisfaction. If you know the ultimate result of what you are doing, you will not lack aspiration. You lose aspiration because you do not remember all the time what aspiration can do for you. People pray for two days, two months, two years, and then they totally forget the goal. But this is not enough. You have to pray for twenty years. When you use a stove, you have to turn the handle to a particular point before the fire comes on. But if you start turning it and do not continue, then there will be no fire at all. So here also your aspiration has to come to a particular point; then only will it give you realisation.

A heart of aspiration
And a mind of determination
Receive special
Fondness-Blessings
From God.

Look at the strength of an iota of aspiration! It has the power to make us feel that God the Infinite is absolutely ours. And something more: that God's infinite Love, Peace, Joy and Power are for our constant use.

Aspiration becomes monotonous after a few years. Instead of climbing up the tree, people descend. So what you have to do is feel what aspiration will bring you. If you look at the thing that is after aspiration, which is realisation, then naturally you will want to fully prepare yourself, energise yourself, inundate yourself with aspiration. So always look one step ahead; look one step ahead to realisation Then you will not be wanting in aspiration. You will be flooded with aspiration.

Do not allow
Your mind's clouds
To hover over
Your heart's aspiration-tree.

If you sincerely dig deep within, your heart's aspiration-spring will not be able to hide anymore.

You can discover your divine qualities by digging deep within. As a miner digs and gets something, you also can dig. Digging here means your inner cry. When you cry, you dive deep within. In order to discover your divine qualities, you have to cry constantly. Each time you cry, you dig deep within; and when you dig deep within, you develop your qualities. So, at every moment, please think of the instrument that digs inside you. It is your aspiration. Just as a miner uses an implement to dig in the ground, you also need a constant inner cry to dig in your heart.

Two are the gifts
Of man's sterling faith:
He cannot live
Without God's Satisfaction,
And God cannot live
Without his aspiration.

My God and my Lord, appreciation from without titillates the human in me. Aspiration from within energises the divine in me. O give me my aspiration-nectar and not my appreciation-poison.

We aspire. Why do we aspire? If we aspire to become great, then our aspiration is not the real aspiration. If we aspire to become good, then our aspiration is real divine aspiration. Goodness is the aim of true aspiration. Greatness alone is constant competition. There is no satisfaction in it. By competition alone we can never achieve satisfaction. But if we become good, if we become divine instruments of God, then we achieve satisfaction far beyond our imagination's flight.

Before, he begged
For satisfaction-alms.
Now he is ready to be satisfied
Simply with aspiration-alms.

As long as your heart remains an ever-mounting aspiration-flame, it makes no difference what your weaknesses are.

Once a seeker has discovered aspiration in the inmost recesses of his heart, all his problems are solved. All past, present and future problems put together are helpless in the face of aspiration, for aspiration is the burning, glowing flame within. It is a birthless and endless flame that mounts high, higher, highest and purifies the things that have to be purified in our unlit, obscure, impure nature. While illumining the unlit, obscure, impure qualities in us, it immortalises the divine qualities in us: faith in God, love of God and unconditional surrender, which say to God, "Let Thy Will be done."

God's Affection-Light
Every day
Blessingfully and powerfully waters
His heart's aspiration-plants.

February

Earthly Happiness
and
Heavenly Bliss

God is all Bliss.

When you have joy, that joy is in the central being, in the heart itself. When you are really joyful, that joy usually remains inside the heart with utmost confidence. Inner joy means real inner security. But if you are happy, it can be on a much lower plane of consciousness—on the physical plane, the vital plane, or the mental plane. Happiness is like a bird that can only spread its wings. Joy is a bird that can fly from the heart. Joy is superior to happiness. Bliss is much higher, much superior to joy. It is infinitely superior to both joy and happiness. There is no comparison. If you can experience bliss, you become immortal. It is something from a much higher plane of consciousness.

Today I shall make myself supremely happy.
Like the morning sun,
I shall flood my body with compassion,
I shall flood my vital with concern,
I shall flood my mind with simplicity,
And I shall flood my heart with purity.

Either you swim in the sea of soulful delight, or you will be caught in the grip of destruction-depression.

To perfect our human life, by far the greatest necessity is our soul's delight. When we live in the physical, the teeming clouds of desire are natural, necessary and inevitable. When we live in the soul, the ever-mounting flames of aspiration are natural, necessary and inevitable.

My Supreme Lord,
What is the difference
Between happiness and delight?
"My child,
Happiness is an experience
And delight is a reality
That transcends experience."

If you are loyal only to God's Love, then happiness will be your only name within, without, below, above.

Joy is in the physical plane. Bliss is in the inner plane, but it is centered around something specific. Delight, with its immortal light, runs throughout the entire being. An unaspiring person can have joy, but he cannot have divine bliss or delight. Only a seeker can experience bliss and delight. Bliss is Infinity. Delight is Immortality's freedom flying constantly in Infinity's sky.

Drown your own glory
If you want a life of peace.
Frown at your own victory
If you want a heart of delight.

For a true seeker there is only one way to be happy: by pleasing his Beloved Supreme.

Ecstasy is something which we usually feel in our higher emotional or illumined vital. Bliss is something we feel in our aspiring, devoted heart. We also feel bliss in the searching mind. Delight is something we feel from the soles of our feet to the crown of our head; it is the entire being that enjoys delight. Delight we feel throughout the body when we are totally dedicated and when we listen unconditionally to the dictates of the Supreme.

I am happy only twice:
Once when I place my loving heart
At the Feet of my Beloved Supreme,
Once when I command my fleeting thoughts
To obey His Will.

From now on I will have no happiness unless I champion the right to be entirely and constantly God's, God's alone.

If we offer our existence to God, to Truth, to Light, then we can expect peace, light and bliss in boundless measure. If we study hard in school, naturally we will expect a high mark. As we sow, so we reap. If we sow divine seeds, seeds of aspiration, then sooner or later we are bound to see the bumper crop of God-realisation. If we can offer our inner cry, if we can cry for peace, light and bliss, then God is bound to come. Our cry will be fulfilled by God, who is the possessor of infinite Peace, Light and Bliss.

Search for the source
Of your smile.
You will see that the source
Is God's own Aspiration-Cry.

He who has wisdom, light and delight will never be caught in the world's unhappiness-net.

We must cherish positive thoughts, positive ideas, positive ideals. Only then will our Goal no longer remain a far cry. Each man has to feel, "I am at the Feet of God, my own Master. I am in the Hands of God, my own Creator. I am in the Heart of God, my only Beloved."

How I wish to be happy today.
O my vital,
At least for one day
Do not discourage others.
O my mind,
At least for one day
Do not emphasise the negative forces
In others.

I give Him what I have and what I am: ignorance. He, out of His infinite Compassion, gives me what He has and what He is: Delight in infinite measure.

In delight alone can an aspirant be true to his inmost self. In delight alone can he feel and understand what God is like. Men speak of God twenty-four hours a day, but not even for a fleeting second do they feel Him, not to speak of understanding Him. If the outer life of an individual can swim in the sea of his soul's delight, then only will he feel God's Presence, and understand Him in His cosmic Vision and absolute Reality.

I am learning something
Most important about delight.
Delight is the unparalleled
Transcendental Beauty
Of God's Satisfaction-Heart.

Divine surrender is delight, constant delight.

To make oneself every day an object of total dedication and surrender is the highest form of bliss. Bliss comes when "I and mine" and "Thou and Thine" leave us for good. Only when we can say that God is ours and we are God's can bliss come. Then, when we feel that God is manifesting in and through us, we get greater bliss. And finally, when we feel that we exist to please God and God alone, when we feel that we came into the world only to please God, then the greatest bliss dawns in our devoted and surrendered heart.

You are aspiring to grow.
Indeed, this is a happy experience.
You are searching for truth.
Indeed, this is a happier experience.
You are surrendering your earth-existence
To the life of delight.
Indeed, this is the happiest experience.

Joy alone has the capacity to shorten our way to God-realisation.

You can maintain your joy permanently when you feel that the joy you are having is not yours. It does not come because you have done something for yourself or for God or for humanity. No! You have to feel that it is an unconditional gift from the Supreme. Then you have to feel that the joy you are experiencing is nothing other than the Supreme Himself. The Supreme has come to you in the form of Joy; so because the Supreme is permanent and eternal within you, your joy is also permanent.

Because your heart believes
In a higher ground
God has cheerfully granted your life
A joyful sound.

A joyful God-seeker will definitely be able to meet with God the playful Lover.

Try to feel that the Supreme has given joy to you not because of what you have done but because He loves you. It is not a result of your action but something that the Supreme Himself wants to give you. Then when you are experiencing this joy, you have to feel that it is not joy as such but the Supreme Himself that you are enjoying. It is not that He has sent you joy and He is somewhere else. No, He Himself has come to you in the form of Joy. If you have this kind of inner awareness, you will be able to maintain your joy permanently, for He who has come to you as Joy is permanent and infinite. If you can see and feel Him as infinite Joy, then your joy will remain permanent.

Do you want to be happy?
Then look at God's Compassion-Eye.
Do you want God to be happy?
Then feel God's Oneness-Heart.

Yesterday I was happy because I faithfully followed my own star. Today I am happy because I bravely live my own life. Tomorrow I shall be happy because I shall unconditionally listen to and fulfil my Beloved Supreme.

I can help my soul to smile more often by becoming a conscious instrument, a devoted and surrendered instrument of God, the Inner Pilot. Now how can I do this? How can I become a devoted instrument? I can become a devoted instrument by remembering what I was once upon a time and what I have now become. That does not mean that I will always dig into my past. Only for a second I shall try to recollect what I was twenty years ago and what I have become. Who has made me what I am now? It is God within me, through my soul, who has done it. When I know this, then automatically gratitude comes to the fore. If I can offer gratitude to God, then He increases my power of dedicated service, love, devotion and surrender.

O my soul, smile!
Smile once more.
Your smile is my only tranquilizer
With no side-effects.
O my soul, smile!

Just as the sun is the only remedy for dark clouds in the sky, similarly, there is no other medicine for our troubled hearts than aspiration.

My joy is my established faith in the Supreme. Unlike others who do not have faith in the Supreme, I do not think and feel that I am always wrong, meaningless and useless. To be sure, those who are wanting in faith are the victims of frustration. To them, life is a barren desert, God is a colossal daydream, death is a roaring lion right in front of them.

My Lord, are You ever sick
Of my complaints?
"No, I am not.
But I AM sick
Of your constant feeling
Of unworthiness."

Here is the secret of my happiness: I keep the mouth of my little self closed and the heart of my big Self open.

Be happy. Do not complain. Who complains? The blind beggar in you. When you complain, you dance in the mire of ignorance-condition. When you do not complain, all conditions of the world are at your feet, and God gives you a new name: aspiration.

My sweet Lord Beloved Supreme,
Do give me the capacity
Not to criticize the world anymore.
Do give me the capacity
To better myself every day
And thus inwardly, secretly and sacredly
Try to serve the world for its improvement.

What can meditation do? It can stop the final victory of sorrow.

We can have the inner experience of bliss if we can acquire the inner silence and if we can have the inner guidance. The inner silence is the silence of goalless movement and thought-waves. The outer silence is the silence of the physical senses. The inner guidance is like a mother's constant and conscious guidance of a child. The outer guidance is like the guidance of a blind man leading another blind man.

Your mind's climbing prayer
And your heart's glowing meditation
Can easily save you.
Your life need not remain
Forever paralyzed
By helpless hopelessness.

Like your heart, you can be happy only when you ask God how things can be done in God's own Way.

The inner experience of bliss is never and can never be a gift of the miracle-machine. The inner experience of bliss is a gift of the natural self of a normal man. The inner experience of bliss begins in self-offering and ends in God-becoming.

I have only four tasks
To perform:
Smile, fly, dive and run.
I have only three tasks
To perform:
Smile, fly and dive.
I have only two tasks
To perform:
Smile and fly.
I have only one task
To perform:
Smile.

FEBRUARY 16

Look at your heart-flower and smile. You will be able to solve your most pressing problems.

Without bliss, man is an external superficiality. With bliss, man is a fulfilling inner and outer reality. Without bliss, man is a song of frustration and destruction. With bliss, man is constant fulfilment and constant perfection.

> *O my seeker-friend,*
> *Your perennial doubt-dilemma will last*
> *Unless you take shelter*
> *In the heart of your self-giving peace.*

You will be happy only when you know that you are not what you appear to be: a lifeless cry and a soulless smile.

What you need is divine joy. God will give you divine joy when you feel that the entire world is a playground where you can play, sing and dance. In God's playground you sing and dance to fulfil and to manifest God. There is no vital pleasure, no vital excitement in this dance; it is the expression of the individual soul in the cosmos. Each soul plays its part to fulfil the Divine in collectivity.

Unreservedly
Change yourself internally.
Unconditionally
Enjoy yourself delightfully—
Today, tomorrow and every day.

Do you want to be happy? Then make your life as soulfully simple as sleeplessly breathing.

When we misuse our time, the after-effects of that incident often turn into suffering. But again, if we go deep within, we will see that it is not suffering as such; it is something else. It is an experience. If we are conscious of it, we become part and parcel of the experience that the Inner Pilot is having. Otherwise, we may feel that suffering is something that is thrust upon us which we do need. For a seeker of the Ultimate Truth, suffering is an experience. At times it is a necessary experience, at times it is not. It depends on what we have done or what experience we have unconsciously invited or invoked. The experience we see in our outer life is an unconscious or conscious expression of our inner purification.

You can be happy
Easily, effectively and permanently
If you can think and feel
That you are of the transcendentally
Beautiful thing, God,
And you are for the universally
Fruitful thing, God.

What is depression? A strong undivine power that destroys the very breath of joy.

Joy is a form of perfection. Perfection and divine joy, inner joy, supreme joy, are inseparable. If you are perfect, you are joyful; and if you are really joyful, cheerful, soulful, then naturally you will be perfect. The spiritual term we use for joy is delight. Since the ultimate Source is delight, naturally delight is perfection. So delight and perfection are always inseparable.

You can be happy
If you say good-bye
To useless thoughts.
Do it, and see if I am correct.

You can be happy
If you say good-bye
To the soulless mind.
Just try it, and see if I am correct.

Nurse no extravagant hope. Your heart will be supremely happy. Feed no malignant doubt. Your mind will be immediately happy.

My Lord Supreme does not want to know what I have done for Him. He just wants to know how I am. If He hears from me that I am happy, then He Himself becomes exceedingly happy. In unmistakable terms He tells me that my happiness is His real and only Satisfaction.

My Beloved Supreme,
How can I be constantly happy?
"My child,
Renounce the desire
To be widely known."

Do not drag your doubt and despair into your aspiration-life if you ever want to become God's sacred ambassador on earth.

Do you want to be happy? If so, then conquer yourself. Do you want to be happier? If so, then do not even think of conquering others. Do you want to be the happiest person on earth? If so, then pray to God soulfully and meditate on God calmly to conquer you and each and everyone in His entire creation at His choice hour.

> *Dogs get joy*
> *By barking and biting.*
> *Men get joy*
> *By fighting and stabbing.*
> *Earth gets joy*
> *By struggling and suffering*
> *Heaven gets joy*
> *By dreaming and smiling.*
> *Seekers get joy*
> *By loving and surrendering.*
> *God gets joy*
> *By illumining and fulfilling.*

Be pleased with yourself constantly. God will grant you His Blessing-Pride regularly.

You were not happy in a human family. Therefore, you are looking for a divine family. Needless to say, this is the only family where happiness will always reign supreme. And the members of this family are a blossoming faith, a surrendering life and a God-pleasing heart.

Do you want to be happy?
Then do not allow yourself to be caught
By your unaspiring heart,
Your unhappy vital
And your God-ignoring body.

**Our departing friends are anxiety and worry, defeat
and disappointment, darkness and ignorance.**

Anxiety and worry we call our friends precisely
because we unconsciously cherish them. It is the
height of folly, but we do cherish them. We cherish
them, therefore they are our friends.

Defeat and disappointment surround our departing friends. Defeat and disappointment shatter our
being; nevertheless we cherish them unconsciously.
Darkness envelopes us, ignorance constantly assails
us. We wallow in the pleasures of ignorance. As long
as they are with us we cherish them, we call them
our friends. But there comes a time when darkness
and ignorance disappear. By virtue of our aspiration or inner cry we liberate ourselves from these
so-called friends: anxiety, worry, defeat, disappointment, darkness and ignorance. Our lasting friends
are hope, determination, faith, personal effort, aspiration and realisation.

*Now that you have regained
Your old dependence on God,
You are bound to become
Once more happy.*

I am happy, genuinely happy, not because God is mine but because I am God's and God's alone.

Self-transcendence brings us the message of happiness. We are happy when we fulfil ourselves in our own way. But when we fulfil ourselves in God's own Way, then we are infinitely more happy. We fulfil our self-imposed duty and thereby we derive joy. But there is something called God-ordained duty. When we fulfil our God-ordained duty we get joy in boundless measure.

I am happy
Not because
I have seen the Face of God,
Not because
I have felt the Heart of God,
But because
God is happy with His Creation-child.

You can transform the hurtful pressures of your life into delightful pleasures just by telling yourself that the world around you can easily exist and even prosper without you.

Sometimes we become very haughty and proud; we are assailed by ego. Again, sometimes we think very ill of ourselves. We go from one extreme to another. This moment we feel that we can break and build the world with our ego-power, and the next moment we feel that we do not have the energy even to budge an inch. We feel that we are hopeless, we are absolutely the most useless person on earth. Then frustration kills us. This moment ego takes us very high, like a balloon, but the next moment it bursts. We do not want to be carried by the ego-balloon, which will burst, and we do not want to allow ourselves to be devoured by the frustration-dragon. So what shall we do? We shall increase our oneness, our inner confidence and assurance. These are the things that will help us to reach our goal.

God has the capacity
To mend your broken heart,
But do you have
The eagerness and willingness
To come to God?

If you have the courage to free your mind from teeming doubts, the Light that never fails shall befriend you before long.

A seeker eventually learns that what he once called suffering is not actually suffering; it is only an experience. There are some experiences in life which are helpful to him in growing into his own ultimate divinity. He is making a mistake if he takes suffering as something which is standing in his way, if he wonders why he has to go through all kinds of suffering. He should feel that it is an experience. He should feel that the inner being is having an experience in and through him either for his outer life's purification or for some inner purification. He should show the world around him that this is something necessary in his life, that through untold suffering, eventually light will dawn.

> *Smile, humanity, smile!*
> *God not only loves you*
> *Constantly*
> *But also needs you*
> *Unreservedly.*
> *Smile, humanity, smile!*

Now that you have destroyed the shackles of the finite, you will be able to sail in the river that flows towards Infinity's ocean of Bliss.

Suffering is not the ultimate message. Happiness and delight are the ultimate message. Delight is our source. Here in the world arena we are given limited freedom. When we misuse this limited freedom we create more suffering, more bondage for ourselves. Instead we can use our limited freedom in a divine way.

*If you are intent
On transformation-light,
Then never be out of
God's inner circle of Delight.*

How can you be happy unless you daily examine and perfect your heart's aspiration-life?

High, higher and highest is the plane of delight. With our illumined consciousness, we rise into that plane and become self-enraptured. Having crossed the corridors of sublime silence and trance, we become one with the Supreme.

From Delight we came into existence,
In Delight we grow.
At the end of our journey's close,
Into Delight we retire.

March

Will-power
and
Determination

MARCH 1

In the ordinary human life, when we are determined to do something, we maintain our determination for five minutes and then all our determination is gone. If we try to achieve determination on our own, it will not last. But once we know what the soul's will-power is, we see that it lasts for many years, even for a lifetime.

The difference between determination and divine will-power is this: determination is in the mind; divine will-power is in the soul. Because the mind is very, very limited, mental determination is not enduring; it is all fluctuation. Mental determination is constantly being destroyed since the mind accepts different ideas at every moment. But the will of the soul is everlasting, ever-progressing and ever-fulfilling because it is one with the Will of the Supreme.

Every day cultivate adamantine will
In the depths of your heart
So that with no difficulty you can bestride
All your problems in the mental world.

A heart of determination is a son of God's achievement-glorification.

Determination ultimately comes from the soul. When we use this power on the physical, vital or mental plane—that is to say, on the outer plane—we call it determination. But when we use it on the inner or psychic plane, we call it will-power, the light of the soul. "Will-power" is the spiritual term that we use for determination. When the light of the soul enters into the vital, we can have one-pointed determination. This one-pointed determination is divine determination, real will-power.

Always take one more step
Than you intended to.
You can, without fail, do it.
Lo, you have done it.

If we make a conscious effort to identify with our soul's will and with the determination of our inner being, only then can our efforts have power.

Divine determination automatically comes if we meditate on the heart's light. Each seeker can develop the capacity to bring light to the fore. If we meditate somewhere else rather than on the heart, our determination may fluctuate. Suppose we are determined to get up the next morning at five o'clock. Tomorrow we may get up at five o'clock with greatest difficulty. But the day after tomorrow, we simply forget to get out of bed. We have not made a determined promise and so we get up at eight o'clock or ten o'clock. Why? Because we have not charged our battery. If we get divine light from our soul during our meditation and if we sincerely pray to the soul to wake us up at five o'clock, then the soul will be pleased. The soul will get us up. It is the soul that can take the responsibility to do what is necessary on our behalf.

My determination
Paired with God's Compassion
Can easily smash the pride
Of impossibility.

MARCH 4

Will is myself. Will is my Self. My Will is absolutely God's and God's alone.

Divine surrender, from the spiritual point of view, comes from will-power. If we have an adamantine will, then we will get the capacity to make unconditional surrender. Again, if we can surrender unconditionally to God, then we will get the capacity to develop will-power. Inner will-power, which is the soul's light, and surrender, which is the oneness of our heart with the Absolute, always go together. They are inseparable.

> *God will be proud of you*
> *If you can tell yourself*
> *That there is no such thing*
> *As failure.*
> *God will love you infinitely more*
> *If you can accept any so-called failures*
> *As experiences*
> *He Himself is having*
> *In you and through you.*

No path can be too hard for you if you have one God-gift: faith in yourself.

A temptation is nothing but a kind of test. If we pass these tests, we become one with God. At first, God will only watch and observe. If, on the one hand, we say outwardly that we do not want to stay with ignorance, but on the other hand, we secretly enjoy wallowing in earthly pleasures, then God simply keeps quiet. But if God sees that we are sincerely trying to pass our examination, then immediately He will give us the capacity.

What is temptation?
Temptation is something
That unconsciously helps
The divine within us
To conquer the human in us.

Any method of spiritual discipline will have two inevitable and inseparable wings: absolute patience and firm resolution.

Whoever wants to give up the spiritual life just because he is not making considerable progress or because he is falling down from time to time, is making a terrible mistake. After accepting the spiritual life, if you consciously leave it, then hostile forces torture you most ruthlessly and the divine forces show considerable indifference. If you do not accept the spiritual life, wonderful. Sleep, sleep; the time has not yet come for you to wake up. But if you already have started to run, and then you go again to sleep, at that time ignorance comes and covers you totally.

God will not be there to receive you
If you hurriedly reach
Your life's finish line.
He will not only receive you
But also garland you and embrace you
If you slowly, steadily and soulfully reach
Your life's finish line.

We have to practice self-discipline if we want to become an instrument of God.

If we want to dive into the inner life, if we want to be guided and moulded by the soul, then we have to be extremely strong. The strength we need is not so much physical strength, but the strength of self-discipline, the strength of self-enquiry, the strength of self-withdrawal from the life of the senses, the strength of self-effacement in the world of offering and self-fulfilment in the world of aspiration and meditation.

Spirituality
Without difficulty
Is an absurdity.

Failure is something that is urging us on to our own realisation. For what we call failure, in God's Eye, is only an experience

In our day-to-day life, when we fail in something we feel that the whole world is lost. We find it extremely hard to bury our sad experience in oblivion. When we succeed, at times we are bloated with pride. We cherish this pride because of our ego. At times we exaggerate our achievement beyond imagination. At times we want to prove to the world that we have or we are something when, in the purest sense of the term, it is not true. We try to make others feel we are exceptional, but in the inmost recesses of our heart, we know that this is false. When we care for progress, we want to be only what God wants us to be. We do not want any appreciation whatsoever from the world. We do not want the world to overestimate or underestimate us; we want the world just to accept us.

You have tried today,
And you have failed.
But tomorrow you will not fail,
Because you are now begging God
To try for you.

Depend on the Grace of the Supreme. To depend on human capacity is stupidity. When we succeed, we call it our capacity, but there is no such thing as human capacity. It is only the divine Compassion acting in and through human capacity. It is all Grace from above.

There are some seekers who feel, "If I care for God's Grace, what necessity is there to make personal effort?" But they are mistaken. Personal effort will never stand in the way of God's descending Grace. Personal effort expedites the descent of God's Grace. God's Grace does not negate personal effort. True, God can give us all that He wants without even an iota of personal effort on our part. But God says, "It is for your pride that I ask you to make this little personal effort."

If you refuse to try,
That means you are deliberately ruining
A lifetime of opportunity.

No will-power, no success. No will-power, no progress.

Will-power is an ever-progressive and self-manifesting reality in the universe. At times we mortals find it difficult to separate our willing from our wishing. We want to achieve our goal with determined personal efforts, supported and guided by God's loving Grace. Whenever we will to achieve something, we pay the price; whereas when we wish to achieve something, very often we do not pay the price: we just wish. Here there is no effort, no conscious effort; and so we can hardly expect any success.

A man of determination
Can easily prove to the world
That he is not a slave
To imperfection-monarch.

MARCH 11

When my inner will energises my outer existence, all my imponderable troubles and excruciating pangs dissolve into thin air.

Try to feel that all your strength, all your determination and will-power is in one particular place, here inside your heart. Feel that you do not exist at all except in this tiny place. You do not have eyes, you do not have a nose, you do not have anything. Intensity will come only when you feel that your entire existence is concentrated at one particular place and not scattered.

Your soulfully patient
Persistence-tears
Are bound to win
God's supreme Smiles.

Although regularity in spiritual practice may appear mechanical, it is a constant blessing from above and shows the development of some inner strength.

Self-discipline is a most important thing in our spiritual life. Even in the ordinary life it is necessary. If a student is not disciplined, then he will not do well in school. And in the spiritual life, if one is not self-disciplined, then God-realisation will remain a far cry.

Tiredness is
Another name for laziness.
Readiness is
Another name for fullness.

Obstructions loom large within and without. Nevertheless, like a kite I shall rise without fail against the wind.

How can you discipline yourself? Through concentration on the things you want most in life. There are very few things on earth we should feel we really need, but unfortunately we are cherishing everything and everyone around us. What we must cherish is truth, light, peace and bliss. If you concentrate on truth, inner truth, then it is truth that will come to the fore in you. Truth can come to you in the form of divine peace or divine light or divine power, but if you really concentrate on the inner truth, automatically and spontaneously truth will come to you.

Only one competition
I appreciate, admire and adore,
And that competition
Is my daily self-transcendence
In God's own Way.

Will-power reaches the goal not because it is the possessor of an adamantine heart, but because it is the boundless lover of an illumining and fulfilling goal.

If you feel the necessity right now of having thousands and millions of things from life, try to minimise your needs. You will see that, while you are in the process of minimising your needs, your life will automatically become disciplined. When you do not give countless outer things your attention, you will see that truth is looking right at you and giving you the strength to discipline your life.

To be a perfect God-lover
A life of temptation
Is a totally foreign language.

How to conquer despair? Never cry for outer consolation. Ever cry for inner compassion. Inner compassion is the flood of light. It is also the flood of perfection's realisation.

The best way to discipline oneself is to pay attention only to the things that are of real need, that are of importance in the inner life. In the outer life we cry for name, fame and many things. Then immediately we are besieged by worries, anxieties and fears. But in the inner life we cry only for God's Concern and God's Compassion. If we will try to feel God's Concern and God's Compassion, then we will see that our life is becoming disciplined.

Do not give up.
If you persist,
Tomorrow's peace will come
And feed your mind today,
And tomorrow's perfection will come
And touch your life today.

There is only one way to get your emotions under control, and that way is to be the conscious expression of your express will- power.

Unfortunately, we are living in an age when self-control is not appreciated; it has become an object of ridicule. A man will be trying hard for self-mastery while his friends, neighbours, relatives, acquaintances and the rest of the world mock him. They find no reason for his sincere attempt to master his life. They think the uncontrolled way they are living this life is far more worthwhile, and that the man who is trying to control his life is a fool, wasting his time and giving up all his joy.

> *Do not blame God!*
> *Demand more*
> *Of yourself.*
> *Do not blame yourself!*
> *Expect less of others.*

To conquer my doubts is to grow into the breath of my will.

Who is the fool: he who wants to have control of his life or he who wants to remain a constant victim to fear, doubt and anxieties? Needless to say, he who wants to conquer himself is not only the wisest man, but the greatest divine hero, the divine warrior. He fights against ignorance in the battlefield of life to establish the Kingdom of Heaven here on earth.

Enthusiasm
Rules his inner world.
Determination
Rules his outer world.
Therefore
Happiness has become
His real name.

Will-power inspires me and energises me to grow into the immediacy of the Eternal Now.

In your spiritual life you are trying to conquer your lower vital. Either today or tomorrow, in the near future or in the most distant future, you are bound to conquer the lower vital. But in the process of your self-transformation, if people do not understand you and do not care for your pure life, please do not pay any attention to their criticism or mockery. If they do not appreciate your sincerity, your attempt and your success in controlling your life, no harm. If you want them to appreciate you and admire your efforts, then you will unnecessarily bring into your life their criticism, their mockery, their doubts and their temptations.

Because you are forceful
Nothing can discourage you.
Because you are faithful
Nobody can defeat you.

He who procrastinates cannot be a true member of God's God-Satisfaction-Family.

Determination is of paramount importance. Each time we are determined, we expedite our journey. In the battlefield of life, with determination we march fast, very fast, towards our Destined Goal.

Personal effort is also of paramount importance. Unless and until we give to the world at large what we have and what we are, we cannot grow into the all-widening and all-embracing Reality—the Reality which we call the Universal Consciousness of the Transcendental Height. Personal effort is founded upon the unconditional Compassion of the Supreme. What we call effort is actually a result of the Supreme's Grace, which rains constantly on our devoted heads and surrendered hearts.

You may see the sun set
On your yesterday's failures
If you want to.
But you must see the sun rise
On your today's determined effort.

A hero-seeker never, never surrenders to his despair-fate. He has heard the inner message that in the battlefield of life, he will eventually win.

We have to know that if our consciousness is low, immediately we can stop our bad thoughts with our will-power. And if we have good thoughts, with our will-power we can strengthen them. Will-power can easily destroy our bad thoughts and negate the wrong forces in us. And with will-power also we can increase the power of our good thoughts and increase our good qualities. So if we use our will-power properly, we can perform miracle after miracle in our lives.

I shall tolerate the world,
I shall.
Only by tolerating the world
Shall I be able to help
My mind to ascend
And
My heart to transcend.

Human will-power is like a rope of sand. At any moment it can break. Divine will-power is the aspiring humanity within us evolving into the all-fulfilling Beyond.

With will-power we realise God. With determination we can perhaps win an outer race. Determination comes from the vital or mind. Will-power comes from the central being. Will- power is infinitely more powerful than determination. If you use your determination, then immediately it can be followed by frustration. But if you use will-power, then all around that will-power and inside that will-power you will see God's Compassion.

Begin again and again
If you really want to win
God's Satisfaction-Heart.

As my inner will is, in the inner world of realisation, so is my outer life, in the world of manifestation.

The best way to develop will-power is through union with God's Will. Daily there may be many unpleasant happenings in your life. If you can accept them cheerfully, then you can increase your will-power. Again, you can increase your will-power by not being affected by the results of your actions. If something takes place, always try to see the positive side of the story. If you can always offer this cheerful attitude, then you will develop will-power.

*Do not think
That you cannot do it.
Just think that God
Is definitely going to do it
In you, for you.*

As soon as you have conquered a difficulty, you will find that it repeats itself on a higher and subtler level. It is the same essential weakness in yourself which you are made to face in a more refined form.

Why do you have to accept defeat, or let us say, failure-life? No, you can be more disciplined, more active, more dynamic, more sincere to reach your goal. And today's goal you will transcend tomorrow. You do not have to accept your limited capacities or your incapacities. Accepting your fate means that you will have no inspiration, no aspiration. Then you will become a perfect friend of lethargy.

Do not accept failure!
If you accept failure
You are lowering yourself
In your own estimation.
An act like that
Is an unconscious suicide.

We shall not fail. On the strength of our inner cry, on the strength of our inner mounting flame, we shall succeed.

The quality which we call determination in our day-to-day life is called will-power in the inner or spiritual world. Real will-power comes from the inmost recesses of our heart, where the soul is located. It is not the product of the physical mind; it comes directly from the soul. The soul's light operates in our outer life as will-power to achieve or manifest something on earth. And this soul's will-power is full of divine humility, which comes directly from the Supreme.

Prosperity
Has made my heart beautiful.
Adversity
Is making my life powerful.

The difference between thought and will is this: thought hesitantly considers; will instantly ventures.

What can will-power do? Will-power can re-move all our confusion—confusion in the physical, the vital, the mind and the heart. How is it that everyone has not realised God? There is just one reason. It is because of confusion in either the mind, the vital, the physical or in our inner existence. The moment this veil of confusion is removed, we see the golden Face of the Supreme within us.

Fortunately
Today's strikingly incompetent
Man of thought
Will surrender to
Tomorrow's amazingly competent
Man of will-power.

A man of will-power braves all the storms and tempests of life.

What else can will-power do? This will-power, which is the soul's light, can enter into reality sooner than at once. We knock at the door of reality with our sincerity, our purity, our aspiration, our dedication and our devotion. We knock at the door of reality, but it may take a few days or months before this door actually opens for us. But when divine determination, divine will-power, knocks at the door of reality, immediately the door opens wide.

You have tried.
You have not succeeded.
That does not mean
That you will not try anymore.

Try once more!
You will not only succeed
In the life that becomes
But also proceed
In the life that eternally is.

Life means will-power, the will-power that unites God's descending Compassion-Smile with man's ascending aspiration-cry.

Once you use will-power, even for two minutes or five minutes, you get tremendous Compassion, boundless Compassion from Above, and this Compassion is nothing other than Light, divine Light. On the physical, vital and mental planes we use determination. On the inner, psychic, soul's plane we use will-power.

Do at least one thing good
In this lifetime
Instead of only becoming
An encyclopedia of good intentions.

Sincerity without the fiery determination for self-improvement is only a beautiful flower with no fragrance at all.

The sincere seeker has to be extremely alert all the time, for the forces of the lower vital can easily rob him. Until God-realisation dawns, he can always be tempted, and can easily swerve from the path of Truth and Light. The very nature of the outer world is temptation. In order to overcome temptation, the seeker has to be constantly vigilant, and always abide by the dictates of the inner will, not by the suggestions of the outer world.

Do not surrender to struggles.
Your ultimate and only goal
Is peace in joy
And joy in peace.
Do not surrender to struggles.

Adversity makes you dynamic. Adversity forces your eyes wide open. Adversity teaches you the meaning of patience. Adversity endows you with faith in yourself. Adversity opens the secret door through which you can see the ultimate future fulfilment of God's Will.

There is no difference between the soul's will- power and unconditional surrender to the Will of the Supreme. Both of them are equally strong. If one can make unconditional surrender to the Will of the Supreme, that means it is the result of one's inner will-power, the soul's light.

A disciplined life
Is a favourite instrument
Of God.

Failure indicates our lack of adamantine determination. Success indicates our tre-mendous power of concentration. Progress indicates that the crown of God's Will is in us and for us.

If you are finding it difficult to discipline yourself to do something, look for the result. If you climb up the tree, then you will get the most delicious fruit. If you do not climb up, you will get no fruits. You know that if someone is disciplined, he can climb up and pluck the most delicious mango and eat to his heart's content. You also can do the same. When you climb up and take the fruit, you get tremendous satisfaction. So by thinking of the satisfaction, you can easily discipline yourself. There is no other way.

Discipline yourself,
Discipline yourself!
Your disciplined life
Will glorify your capacity
And multiply God's Confidence in you.
Discipline yourself,
Discipline yourself!

You must not delay! You must achieve as soon as possible before your life fades away.

No matter how feeble our will-power is in comparison to God's adamantine Will-Power, human will-power will say, "God, I am ready to fulfil You. Please tell me what I should do. I want to be Your instrument. I want to be Your dynamic hero and warrior. My power may be limited, but this limited quantity I am ready to use. Do You want to sit on my shoulder? Then sit. Do You want me to run for You? Then I will run. If You want to bring me something to do, I will do it. On the way I may break my legs, but I will do my best for You." This determination, this will-power, is never, never afraid of doing anything or saying anything. It knows that its strength comes forth from the soul, and the soul has God as its very own.

Keep trying!
It so often happens
That the last key opens the door.
Likewise, it is your last prayer
That may grant you salvation,
And your last meditation
That may grant you realisation.

April

Purity

APRIL 1

Purity is my hidden divinity.

How to be pure? We can be pure by self-control. We can control our senses. It is unbelievably difficult, but it is not impossible. The hungry lion that lives in our senses and the hungry tiger that lives in our passions will not leave us because of the mere repetition of the thought, "I shall control my senses and conquer my passions." This approach is of no avail. Nor is it advisable to always think of our impurity and brood over it. If we meditate on the positive side, that is to say on light, then light is going to descend into us.

What we must do is fix our mind on God. To our utter amazement, the lion and tiger of impurity, now tamed, will leave us of their own accord. To fix our body, mind and heart on the Divine is the right approach. The closer we are to the Light, the farther we are from the darkness.

Your sweetest dreams
Are founded upon
Purity's oneness-heart.

Look at the miracle of a drop of venom and a drop of purity. The former poisons the blood in your veins. The latter purifies the human soul in your body.

Purity does not come all at once. It takes time. We must dive deep and lose ourselves with implicit faith in contemplation of God. We need not go to purity. Purity will come to us. And purity does not come alone. It brings with it an everlasting joy. This divine joy is the sole purpose of our life. God reveals Himself fully and manifests Himself unreservedly only when we have this inner joy.

> *Invite purity's life*
> *On the strength of your sincerity.*
> *Invite divinity's breath*
> *On the strength of your purity-life.*

Purity's breath is the field. Divinity's assur-ance is the plow. Immortality's immortal Smile is the farmer.

You have to aspire for purity in the gross physical. It is the physical in you that needs radical trans-formation and for that what you need is physical purity. Purity in the physical can be established only by bringing down light from above into the physical and lower vital consciousness, especially below the navel centre. How can you do it? It is through constant elevating prayer and constant inner cry for light. Light and darkness cannot stay together; it is impossible. Similarly, purity and impurity cannot stay together. You should meditate on the transcen-dental Light. When light descends into your emo-tional vital and physical body, then automatically, spontaneously, the light will purify the conscious and the unconscious or lower worlds within you.

A heart of purity
Always has the capacity
To shine like the snow-white
And blue-gold peaks
Of aspiration-mountain.

APRIL 4

If you can keep pure thoughts in your mind during the day, then at night you will be blessed with the company of angels.

In our day-to-day life we very often come across people and places that are very impure. While walking along the street a spiritual person may sense tremendous impurity at a particular spot where an ordinary person may not notice anything at all. One can easily be attacked by the impurity of others. The only way to prevent this is by energizing ourselves with the soul's power. The soul's power is always alert and can easily come to our aid.

O purity,
By the very sound of your name
Anything that is attacking me
Is weakened
And my own good qualities
Come to the fore.

When we are pure, we can receive divine Peace, Light, Bliss and Power in abundant measure. When we can maintain our purity, peace, joy, light, bliss and power can dawn on earth.

Purity is the light of our soul expressing its divinity through the body, the vital and the mind. When we are pure we gain everything. If we can retain our purity, we will never lose anything worth keeping. Today we may have great thoughts or great inner power, but tomorrow we are bound to lose them if we are not pure. Purity is the Breath of the Supreme. When purity leaves us, the Breath of the Supreme also leaves, and we are left with only our human breath.

I purify my body
By chanting God's Name.
I purify my vital
By serving God.
I purify my mind
By emptying my mind for God.
I purify my heart
By meditating on God's Compassion-Love.

Let me not lose an iota of purity from my devotion-heart, for purity is the safest and shortest way to reach my Ultimate Goal, complete oneness with my Lord Supreme.

Purity is like a divine magnet. It pulls all divine qualities into us. When we have purity, the world is filled with pride in us. If Mother-Earth houses a single pure soul, her joy knows no bounds. She says, "Here, at last, is a soul I can rely upon."

Simplify your life,
Purify your heart,
Multiply your God-love.
Lo, God is claiming you
As His very own.

Let us be pure, and then we shall immediately learn that we belong to our Beloved Supreme alone, forever and forever.

If you want to have more purity, you can do this spiritual exercise which is most effective. You all know the significance of Aum, the name of God. To start with, on Sunday you will repeat this sacred name of the Supreme one hundred times; Monday, two hundred; Tuesday, three hundred; Wednesday, four hundred; Thursday, five hundred; Friday, six hundred; Saturday, seven hundred. Then on the following Sunday you come down to six hundred; Monday, five hundred; and so on, to four hundred, three hundred, two hundred, one hundred. If you want to establish purity all around you, within and without, then this is the most effective spiritual exercise.

The divinity
Of a purity-heart
Has always to be sought
And invited.

A purity-heart is the author of our blossoming faith.

Prayer is purity. It purifies our mind. The mind is always subject to doubt, fear, worry and anxiety. It is always assailed by wrong thoughts, wrong movements. When we pray, purification takes place in our mind. Purity increases our God-receptivity. In fact, purity is nothing short of God-receptivity.

> *Each impure thought*
> *Is famous in infamy*
> *In the inner world,*
> *And is immediately sent*
> *Into an implacable exile*
> *By purity's adamantine will.*

Where life is pure, inspiration and aspiration are also pure.

Outer cleanliness can be of great help and assistance to inner purity. If we take a shower and put on clean, fresh clothes, the things we are allowing to surround us are already pure and divine. Then it will be easier for us to prevent the undivine, hostile, lower vital forces from entering into us and keep our mind and vital pure and divine.

My Lord,
You have given me
The capacity to cry.
My Lord,
You have given me
The capacity to smile.
Now please give me the capacity
To have purity inside my cry
And beauty inside my smile.

With his purity the seeker makes considerable progress. His heart is pure, his very existence is pure; therefore, he is able to make most satisfactory progress.

Without purity we will not be able to achieve anything substantial in the spiritual life, and we will not be able to maintain the little that we do achieve. But if we have purity, then we can have all the divine qualities in boundless measure. If we have boundless purity, then our inner achievements can last forever. But unless and until we have established solid purity in boundless measure, God-realisation will remain a far cry.

If you bow daily
To your heart's purity-altar,
Then your life will be flooded
With God's Vision-Stars.

If you want guidance, then look up with a pure heart. If you want guidance, then look within with a doubt-free mind.

How do we become pure? One way we acquire purity is by mixing with spiritual people, with pure people. From them we will get inspiration and guidance. The other way is to consciously think of ourselves as children, divine children. If we feel that we are divine children, we know that there is Somebody to take care of us. And who is that? It is our divine Parent. A child has no sense of impurity. He is always pure. If we can always feel that we are divine children, then our sense of impurity will go away and our soul will spontaneously tell us what is the best thing for us. And inside that message purity will loom large.

If you have the capacity
To develop a pure heart,
Then God will feel the necessity
To grant you a supreme boon:
He will give you
His saint-children
To play with.

Because you have a new heart, you will be the possessor of new God-experiences.

Let us be pure. The Supreme will love us. If there is no purity in the aspirant's inner or outer life, then the aspirant is no better than an animal. Without purity he cannot retain any of the spiritual gifts he receives. Everything will disappear and everything will disappoint the seeker if he is wanting in purity. But if he is flooded with purity, the divine qualities will all eventually enter into him. They will sing in him, dance in him and make him the happiest person on earth. And by making him happy, these divine qualities will find their own true fulfilment.

I know
If I become pure,
Absolutely pure,
My Lord Supreme
Will turn me into
His own melody-producing angel.

In the spiritual life, purity is as essential as our very life-breath, and God gives us purity only when we feel that He is our only necessity.

Purity does demand that you have a clean body, but true physical purity lies inside the heart. You have to establish an inner shrine within your heart. This shrine is the constant remembrance of the Supreme Pilot inside you. When you constantly and spontaneously think of the Supreme Pilot seated inside you, in the inmost recesses of your heart, you will realise that this is the highest purity.

Beauty is of various types,
But the beauty of purity
Shall always remain
Unparalleled.

Among all divine qualities, purity is un-paralleled. There is no other quality that can maintain and sustain our divinity.

If purity is lacking in the physical, complete success, the full manifestation of God, cannot be accomplished. You may get partial spiritual success, but even this partial success in life will disappoint you badly if purity is not established in your nature. You have to establish purity in the physical, in the vital, in the mind—everywhere in the outer nature. Then whatever you do, whatever you are, whatever you possess will be filled with purity. Purity is not something weak or negative; it is something soulful and dynamic. It is something that is fed constantly by the infinite Energy and the indomitable, adamantine Will of the Supreme.

Before God grants you
Your liberation,
You will have to pass
His purity-inspection.

If you want to see the hidden treasures of your heart, then first see the Footprints of God in your heart's purity-snow.

The very utterance of the word "purity" can help to change the aspirant's outer life as well as his inner life. Repeat the word "purity" one hundred and eight times daily, placing your right hand on your navel as you say it. Then you will see that abundant purity will enter into you and flow through you. When you are pure, you will see the world with a different eye. You will see purity dawning fast in the world. You will see beauty blooming fast in the world. You will see perfection growing fast in the world.

What has soulful purity
Done for me?
It has richly helped me
To spread my oneness-love
Here, there and all-where.
Try to achieve it.
You, too, will succeed.

To love God I need one thing: purity's breath.

Sweet, sweeter, sweetest is purity. When you see purity inside you, you are pure. When you feel purity inside and around you, you are purer. When you become purity within and without, you are purest. You actually kill your inner being when you lead an impure life. But when you lead a pure life, you expedite the journey of your soul. Your soul and your outer life get their greatest opportunity when purity is totally established in your life.

If you nourish
Your inner purity,
Your outer divinity
Will flourish.

A pure heart can enjoy God's Love for a fleet-ing second, but God's Love enjoys a pure heart forever and forever.

Purity is like muscle that can be built up through exercise and practice. You need many years of practice and also God's Grace. If you try to achieve purity, certainly you will get it. If you do not get it today, you will get it in ten years or in the next incarnation. Total purity in the physical, the vital and the mind takes time. You are crying for purity in the heart. You may get it in a few days or a few months, let us say. But it takes more time to get purity in the mind. In the vital, it is still more difficult. In the physical, God alone knows how many years it takes. Comparatively, it is much easier to get purity inside the heart. The soul is always pure; if you identify with the soul, at that time you are all purity.

O purity, I love you,
For when you come forward
You create beauty's oneness
And divinity's fulness.

Have new inner friends, especially your heart's purity and your soul's divinity.

To have experiences without the strength of purification is like living in the most dangerous part of the forest. This does not mean that experience must always wait for complete purification. What is actually needed is a good understanding and a true relation between growing experience and growing purification.

If you can purify
The quantity of your mind,
You will be able to intensify
The quality of your heart
And satisfy the God-hunger inside you.

True, my heart of purity can alone see the Face of God. Equally true, my heart of impurity is not ignored by God. On the contrary, my heart's impurity is well taken care of by God's constant Compassion.

A supreme contest is going on between purity and impurity in our nature. Water is water, but some water may make us sick if we drink it while other water refreshes and energises us. Truth sees whether the seeker wants the purest water or not. When it is fully convinced that our promise is absolutely sincere, that even if we do not get the inner light immediately, we will not go back to falsehood, that our choice is light and nothing else, it will dispossess falsehood totally.

My purity-heart
Is the priceless gift
From my Absolute Beloved Supreme.

Purity's oneness-life is the world's transcen-dental hope.

There are two qualities that we need most. One quality is purity and the other is oneness. Of course, purity and oneness are inseparable. Purity is on the outer plane of consciousness and oneness is on the inner plane of consciousness. If we want to go from the outer plane of consciousness to the inner plane, then first we will develop purity and from purity we will enter into oneness. But if we want to come from the inside to the outside, which is also correct, then we start with oneness; and when there is oneness, purity is already there. Oneness cannot separate itself from purity.

> *Impurity divides.*
> *Purity unites.*
> *Because God is pure,*
> *He is One;*
> *He is His Heart's Oneness-Song*
> *In His Life's Fulness-Dance.*

APRIL 21

Nothing is as pure as the heart's aspiration.

For mental purity we need tremendous aspiration. Purity is on the outer plane, but once it is established, then we can establish oneness with the inner being. Then we will be perfect. When we have oneness in the inner being and purity in the outer life, automatically we get the capacity for manifestation and become a perfect instrument of the Supreme. At that time, we are not only with the Supreme and for the Supreme, but we are the Supreme. That is what oneness can and will tell us.

Your purity-born aspiration
Will definitely be able to play
With God's Divinity-smiling Face.

Faith and purity are the sunrise of a seeker's heart.

Purity is the light of our soul expressing its divinity through the physical, the vital and the mind. Purity means following the dictates of our Inner Pilot without allowing undivine forces to enter into us. Wherever there is a lack of purity there is obscurity, and obscurity is the pioneer of death. What we call obscurity today, is death for us tomorrow. Purity is the only thing that can sustain our divinity. If there is no purity, there is no certainty. If there is no purity, there is no spontaneity. If there is no purity, there is no constant flow of divinity inside us.

Purity has the capacity
To immediately destroy
Insecurity and pride.
Purity has the capacity
To immediately create
Oneness with God's
Transcendental Will.

Have purity first; then only will you never be devoid of power.

Once purity is established, especially in the vital, much, much is accomplished in one's inner life and outer life. In human purity abides God's highest Divinity. Man's purity is God's Breath. If we have purity we have everything. Purity is tremendous power. We can accomplish anything with purity. But if we lose our purity, although we may have power, wealth or influence, we will crumble, we can easily fall.

Yesterday I fought with God
With my impurity-breath.
Today I am dancing with God
With my purity-heart.

My purity-heart always reveals my soul's hidden promise to my life.

We have to breathe in purity as we breathe in air during our meditation and during our day-to-day activities. We have to think of purity consciously. We have an inner existence and we have an outer existence. Our inner existence is bound to be suffocated when it is impossible for us to breathe in purity. The cosmic Self, the universal Self, is always eager to supply us with purity in infinite measure. If purity is not established in our inner life, our outer life is bound to fail sooner or later. In purity our divinity can grow; in purity our true life can flourish and have its fulfilment here on earth.

Because your heart is pure,
The heart of the world
Has become pure to you.

My mind often feels lost when it sees the purity, beauty and divinity of my heart.

Purity in thought is extremely difficult to attain. Purity in outer action is easier, but purity in thought has to be achieved first. How can we have purity in the mind, in our thoughts and ideas? We can easily have this purity if we feel that we are not the body but the soul. The word "soul" immediately brings purity to our mind in abundant measure. Purity will come to us; it has to come to us the moment we feel that we are not the body but the soul. Even if we do not know what the soul is, the very word "soul" brings to our mind a sense of luminosity, a sense of divinity, a sense of unalloyed joy. And these divine qualities spontaneously give birth to purity.

I imitate.
I want my mind to imitate.
What is the thing
That we are going to imitate?
The thing we are going to imitate
Is the fragrance-rose
Of my purity-heart.

Purity is the ceaseless shower of God's omnipotent Grace on aspiring human souls.

Running considerably helps the seeker to establish purity. Each time he breathes in, if he can remember or repeat just one time God's Name, or "Supreme," or whatever divine name or form comes to his mind, then that spiritual thought will increase his purity. Either it turns into purity within the runner or it grants purity to the runner.

A purity-heart
Is his newly acquired
Inner treasure.

Your heart's purity can easily calm your storm-tossed mind.

Every day in order to perfect your emotional life you have to bring down purity into your system. This purity is the purity of oneness. Begin with oneness with your soul; then try to establish oneness with your heart, then with your mind, then with your vital, then with your body. What you should do is enter into the soul's perfection first and then bring it into the heart. Feel that you have entered into the perfection-river and you are flowing from the soul to the heart. And feel that your aspiration is the river's speed. After you come to the heart, if you feel that you need a little rest because you have already covered such a great distance, you can remain in the heart for a few days or a few months.

The fragrance of my heart's purity
Goes far beyond
My mind's impurity-territory.

The mind is not bad. Just make it pure. You will be able to enjoy the purity-fragrance of truth.

To continue to establish the purity of oneness, when you feel that you are again energetic, use your aspiration-speed, and the perfection-river will start flowing to your mind. Again, if you feel that you have covered a very good distance and need some rest, you can wait indefinitely there. Then, from the mind, you start your journey to the vital, and from there you come to the physical. If you can journey from your soul to your body, you will have perfection in your everyday life, in every sphere of your life. You have to start from the source, the soul.

His meditation-dawn
Has purified the impurity
Of his mind's city.

When your heart thinks for you, you are safe for God is always pleased with your purity-heart.

We can purify the mind either by emptying the mind or by invoking light from above or from within. We can think of the mind as a vessel. The vessel is full of dirty, filthy water, let us say. If we empty it, then only do we get the opportunity to fill it up again with pure water. Or we can think of the mind as a dark room, a room that has not seen light for many, many years. If we take the mind as a dark room, we see that we need someone who can bring light into this room. That person is the soul. So we have to make friends with the soul. We have to invoke this most intimate friend who has the capacity to help us and the willingness to illumine anything that is dark within us. We have to consciously feel that we need the soul just as we need the body. If our need is sincere and genuine, then the soul will come forward and illumine the darkness that we have in our minds.

Delay not, delay not!
You must replace
Your mind's old impurity-life
With your heart's new purity-life.

A childlike purity always obeys the inner voice, and if one obeys the inner voice, then he can be freed from committing mistakes.

You should always pray for purification. All the negative forces will attack you unless and until you are purified. When you pray and meditate, consciously pray or meditate on purity inside the heart first. When purity is well-established there, then all your wrong forces are bound to disappear. Eventually, the undivine forces will not even be able to enter into you.

If you do not develop
More purity in your heart,
Your spiritual life will be
Intensely frustrating.

May

Peace

It is only through inner peace that we can have true outer freedom.

A child finds peace in noise and activity. An adult finds peace when he feels that he can lord it over the world. An old man thinks that he will get peace if the world recognizes his greatness. But peace can never dawn on any individual if it is not properly sought.

A day will come when the child will pray to God for a calm and quiet life. Then he will have peace. If an adult wants to have peace, he has to realise that he cannot get it by possessing the world or governing the world. It is only by offering what he has and what he is, consciously and unreservedly, to the world at large, that he will have peace. The old man can have peace only if he cherishes the idea that he is not a beggar, but a king. He has offered his inner and outer wealth to mankind. If, in the evening of his life, he does not expect anything from the world, then his inner consciousness and outer being will be flooded with peace.

Peace is the beginning of love.
Peace is the completion of truth.
Peace is the return to the Source.

Peace is the perfection of one's mind and the divinization of one's thoughts.

How can we have peace, even an iota of peace, in our outer life, amid the hustle and bustle of our multifarious activities? Easy: we have to choose the inner voice. Easy: we have to control our binding thoughts. Easy: we have to purify our impure emotions. We have to listen to the inner voice always. It is our sure protection. We have to be cautious of the binding thoughts. These thoughts have tremendous vitality. We must never allow them to swell into mountains. We have to face them and then dominate them. These thoughts are absolutely non-essentials. We have to refrain from the luxury of the emotional storm. How can we choose the inner voice? To choose the inner voice, we have to mediate early in the morning. To control and dominate our undivine thoughts, we have to meditate at noon. To purify our unlit, impure emotions, we have to meditate in the evening.

At last,
A moment of peace!
My doubting mind
Has surrendered
To my illumining heart.

If you remain calm and quiet and allow the divine thoughts of your spiritual guide to enter into you, you will become flooded with peace.

Each time you breathe in, try to feel that you are bringing into your body peace, infinite peace. Now, what is the opposite of peace? Restlessness. When you breathe out, please try to feel that you are giving out nothing but the restlessness of your body and mind and the restlessness that you see around you. When you breathe in this way, restlessness will leave you.

When there is no difference
Between you and your heart's
Meditation-sea,
God will grant you
His Peace-Empire.

The greatest misfortune that can come to a human being is to lose his inner peace. No outer force can rob him of it. It is his own thoughts, his own actions, that rob him of it.

Our greatest protection lies not in our material achievements and resources. All the treasure of the world is emptiness to our divine soul. Our greatest protection lies in our soul's communion with the all-nourishing and all-fulfilling peace. Our soul lives in peace and lives for peace. If we live a life of peace, we are ever enriched and never impoverished. Unhorizoned is our inner peace; like the boundless sky, it encompasses all.

Long have we struggled, much have we suffered, far have we travelled. But the face of peace is still hidden from us. We can discover it if ever the train of our desires loses itself in the Will of the Lord Supreme.

Unless you become
The renouncer of expectation,
You cannot be
The possessor of peace.

If you sincerely want peace in the outer world, then offer all your wisdom. If you sincerely want peace in the inner world, then offer all your silence.

We own peace only after we have totally stopped finding fault with others. We have to feel the whole world as our very own. When we observe others' mistakes, we enter into their imperfections. This does not help us in the least. Strangely enough, the deeper we plunge, the clearer it becomes to us that the imperfections of others are our own imperfections, but in different bodies and minds. Whereas if we think of God, His Compassion and His Divinity enlarge our inner vision of Truth. We must come in the fulness of our spiritual realisation to accept humanity as one family.

Secretly God has told me something:
He who argues
Prefers his boastful mind
To his peaceful heart.

A seeker of peace desires beauty within.

We must not allow our past to torment and destroy the peace of our heart. Our present good and divine actions can easily counteract our bad and undivine actions of the past. If sin has the power to make us weep, meditation has undoubtedly the power to give us joy, to endow us with the divine wisdom. Our peace is within, and this peace is the basis of our life. So beginning today, let us resolve to fill our minds and hearts with tears of devotion, the foundation of peace. If our foundation is solid, then no matter how high we raise the superstructure, danger can never threaten us. For peace is below, peace is above, peace is within, peace is without.

If you can open your heart
As a flower to the sun,
God will enfold you,
Your entire being
In His universal Peace.

We can attain lasting inner peace only when we feel that our Supreme Pilot is in the many as one and in the one as many.

Peace comes in and we lose it because we feel that we are not responsible for humanity, or that we are not part and parcel of humanity. We have to feel that God and humanity are like a great tree. God is the tree, and the branches are His manifestation. We are branches, and there are many other branches. All these branches are part of the tree and are one with each other and with the tree. If we can feel that we have the same relationship with God and with humanity as the branch has with its fellow branches and with the tree as a whole, we are bound to get everlasting peace.

As the countless drops
Of the boundless ocean
Or the myriad leaves
Of a huge banyan tree
Peacefully remain side by side,
Even so, all human beings
Will someday live side by side
In a perfect oneness-world.

God has infinite children, but the name of His fondest child is peace.

There is absolutely nothing as important as the search for peace in the outer world. Without peace the outer world is not only wicked to the backbone, but also hopelessly weak. Peace itself is strength. When you have inner peace, you can have joy and delight when you enter into the outer world. The outer world can be under your control when you have peace of mind, even if you have only a little peace of mind. Wherever you go, you will make your own peace. If you do not have any inner peace to offer, the only qualities you will express are restlessness and aggression.

Do you need peace of mind?
Then think that the world does not need you.
Do you need peace of mind?
Then feel that the world
Is not nearly as useless as you think.
Do you need peace of mind?
Then see that you do not make
The same mistakes
That the world quite often makes.

MAY 9

God has peace of mind because He has thrown away expectation.

World peace will begin when the so-called human expectation ends. World peace can dawn only when each individual realises the Supreme Truth: Love is the revelation of life and life is the manifestation of love. World peace can be achieved, revealed, offered and manifested on earth when in each person the power of love replaces the love of power.

My Lord,
You have entered into my heart
And made me feel
That we are all brothers and sisters
Of one world-family.
Now do enter into my mind
So it will act like the heart,
And I will not be able
To hurt others.

What are the things that can inspire us to have peace in the outer world? Simplicity can inspire our body, humility can inspire our vital, sincerity can inspire our mind and purity can inspire our heart.

No price is too great to pay for inner peace. Peace is the harmonious control of life. It is vibrant with life-energy. It is a power that easily transcends all our worldly knowledge. Yet it is not separate from our earthly existence. If we open the right avenues within, this peace can be felt here and now. Peace is eternal. It is never too late to have peace. Time is always ripe for that. We can make our life truly fruitful if we are not cut off from our source, which is the peace of Eternity.

My open-heart policy:
Peace
At any price.

He is mistaken who thinks that peace will, on its own, enter into his life at the end of his life's journey. To hope to achieve peace without meditation and spiritual discipline is to expect water in the desert.

To have peace of mind, prayer is essential. Now, how to pray? With tears in our hearts. Where to pray? In a lonely place. When to pray? The moment our inner being wants us to pray. Why to pray? This is the question of questions. We have to pray if we want our desires or aspirations to be fulfilled by God. What can we expect from God beyond this? We can expect Him to make us understand everything, everything in nothing and nothing in everything: the Full in the Void and the Void in the Full.

Peace. Peace. Peace.
Peace is love unmistakably realised.
Peace is joy unreservedly shared.
Peace is oneness soulfully expanded.
Peace is fulness permanently founded.

If you can remain thoughtless, in the sense that the mind is absolutely calm and quiet, then you will constantly feel peace in bound-less measure.

Peace, the world needs. We all need peace. But when we think of peace we try to discover it in our mind. We feel that peace can be found only in the mind, and if once we can discover peace in the mind, then our problems will be solved for good. But at this point I wish to say that the mind we are referring to is the physical mind. The mind is the doubting mind, and in the doubting mind we can never feel the presence of peace. We can feel the presence of peace only in the loving heart. The doubting mind leads us to total frustration. The loving heart leads us to complete satisfaction.

Ask your mind to be clever.
What your mind needs is peace,
And this peace it can get
Only from one place:
The heart of oneness,
And nowhere else.

Peace begins when expectation ends.

Peace is our inner wealth. The inner wealth we can bring to the fore only when we expect nothing from the outer world and everything from the Supreme Pilot within us, at God's choice Hour. Often, when we work for the world and serve the world we feel that it is the world's bounden duty to offer us gratitude or to acknowledge our service. When we expect something from the world, we are bound to meet with frustration. But when we expect from the Inner Pilot, He fulfils us beyond the flight of our imagination. But one thing we must know, and that is that God has an Hour of His own.

> *The supreme secrets of a peaceful life:*
> *Expect not; just give.*
> *Delegate not; just start and continue.*
> *Retire not; just aspire for self-transcendence.*

The life of peace is the result of our unconditional dedication to the Will of the Supreme. If we do not expect anything from the world, either good or bad, then we will have peace in our entire being.

Our duty is to pray for peace, meditate on peace, concentrate on peace and contemplate on peace. God's duty is to inundate us with His Peace. When we know the art of surrender, the kingdom of peace within us cannot separate itself from our living reality. It is our conscious inner surrender, our unconditional surrender to the Inner Pilot, that expedites our journey towards the discovery of the all-illumining and all-fulfilling Peace.

If you can have
Obedience, obedience, obedience,
Then you can have
A heart-home of peace.

God will give you peace only when you feel that you are not indispensable, either to your family or to the world.

Each individual being, each man and woman, should feel that he or she belongs to all nations. That does not mean that one neglects one's own nation to devote attention exclusively to other nations. But each human being who has the energy and willingness to be of service to other nations will also have the willingness to serve his or her own country in ample measure. While serving one's own country, one has to feel that it is becoming one with other nations. You can do this only when you feel that you have gone far beyond your little family and have accepted the world-family as your very own.

Because of the universality
Of his oneness-heart,
Peace follows him
Wherever he goes.

In the outer life you cannot have peace unless and until you have first established peace in your inner life.

Early in the morning, if you treasure a few divine thoughts before leaving your home, these thoughts will enter into the outer life as energising, fulfilling realities. It is in the inner world that everything starts. The inner world is where we sow the seed. If we sow the seed of peace and love, naturally it will produce a tree of peace and love when it germinates. But if we do not sow the seed, then how are we going to have the plant or the tree? It is impossible! The peace we bring to the fore from the inner world through our prayer and meditation is very strong, very powerful, and it lasts. So when we have that peace in our inner life, the outer life is bound to be transformed. It is only a matter of time.

The inner experience of peace
Is man's supreme necessity.
The inner experience of peace
Is man's transcendental beauty.
The inner experience of peace
Is man's absolute reality.

Early in the evening, between six and seven, is the best time to meditate for peace. Nature, as it offers its salutations to the setting sun, will inspire you, comfort you and help you in achieving peace.

If you want to have inner peace, then you must follow the path of spirituality. Spirituality is the answer. There are three ages of man: under-age, over-age and average. To the under-age, spirituality is hocus-pocus. To the over-age, spirituality is something dry, uncertain and obscure. And to the average, spirituality is self-oblivion, self-negation and self-annihilation. But a true seeker will say that spirituality is something normal, natural, spontaneous, fertile, clear, luminous, divinely self-conscious, self-affirmative and self-creating.

How to be
A consistent peace-lover?
Just try the spiritual life,
Which has and is God,
The all-nourishing Peace.

Aspiration can be raised to meet the peace from above. But peace must be brought down to remove one's difficulties.

Peace you want and need. To have peace, you must have free access to your soul. To have free access to your soul, you must have inner silence. To have inner silence, you need aspiration. To have aspiration, you need God's Grace. To have God's Grace, you must feel that you are God's and God's alone, always!

If you are
A peace-supplier,
Then God will come to you
As a Supreme Lover.

The absence of peace makes one feel that his is the life of an insignificant ant. The presence of peace makes one feel that his is the life for even God to be truly proud of.

What creates restlessness? Restlessness indicates dissatisfaction with what we see and what we have and what we are. If we have peace of mind, anything that we have, anything that we are, anything that we are growing into is enough for us. When there is peace, satisfaction is constantly increasing and inner hunger is also increasing. But when there is restlessness, we will feel there is no satisfaction.

How do we get peace of mind? We get peace of mind only when we feel that there is some higher Authority that is thinking of us, that is showing us His Love, His Concern. If we feel there is somebody far above us who is thinking of us and showing us Concern, Compassion, Love, Blessings, then only does our restlessness go away.

To see
A face of love
Is to feel
A heart of peace.

What can give us peace of mind? Only acceptance of God's Will can give us true peace of mind.

By accepting God's Will as our own, very own, we can get peace. Then only can our life be fruitful. In God's Eye there is no such thing as possession and renunciation. In God's Eye there is only one thing: acceptance—acceptance of God's Will. In our heart, in our life, there is only one ultimate prayer, the prayer that the Saviour Christ has taught us: "Let Thy Will be done." Millions of prayers have been written from time immemorial, but no prayer can equal this one: "Let Thy Will be done." When we accept God's Will as our own, at every moment peace looms large in our life of wisdom, in our life of aspiration and in our life of dedication.

Man's real goal
Is peace.
Peace feeds him,
His life inner and outer.

You and I create the world by the vibrations that we offer to the world. If we can invoke peace and then offer it to somebody else, we will see how peace expands from one to two persons, and gradually to the world at large.

Peace does not mean the absence of war. Outwardly two countries may not wage war, but if they inwardly treasure aggressive thoughts, hostile thoughts, that is as good as war. Peace means the presence of harmony, love, satisfaction and oneness. Peace means a flood of love in the world family. Peace means the unity of the universal heart and the oneness of the universal soul.

Victory and defeat are interwoven.
Do not try to separate them
But try to go beyond them
If your heart longs for abiding peace.

Empty the mind! Lo and behold, right in front of you there is a fountain of peace.

An ordinary person feels that a sea of peace is beyond his reach. But this sea of peace is at his command if he enters and continues to practise the spiritual life. The foundation stone of the spiritual life is peace. In the spiritual life we achieve peace only when we knock at God's Door. If we knock at the door of a human being, then we shall never achieve peace. At every moment we have to feel that we can get peace only from God.

Peace is the gift of gifts
That God bestows
Upon His choice children.

What is peace? Peace is to see God's Beauty.

Peace is man's greatest and highest blessing. Man thinks that he can get everything with prosperity; but if he is wanting in peace, then he is the worst possible beggar. We say "peace of mind" but actually we do not have peace in the mind. By staying in the mind, we can never have even a glimpse of peace. When we want peace, we have to go beyond the realm of the mind. How can we go beyond the mind? It is through our constant aspiration. That aspiration will enable us to collect the mind like a bundle and throw it into the sea of the heart. Then we will see that our mind, vital and physical—our whole existence—will be inundated with inner peace.

Peace-seed must be sown
In the heart.
Only then will it grow
In the body of human life.

To be sure, peace is not the sole monopoly of Heaven. Our earth is extremely fertile. Here on earth we can grow peace in measureless measure.

What are the things that prevent us from acquiring peace in the outer world? Our self- indulgence in the world of the body, our self-aggrandisement in the world of the vital, our self-doubt in the world of the mind and our sense of self-insufficiency in the world of the heart prevent us from acquiring peace in the outer world.

In your outer life
If you long for peace,
Then in your inner life
You must become energy-action.

When you have inner peace, you can have joy and delight when you enter into the outer world.

What are the things that can inspire our body, vital, mind and heart to have peace in the outer world? Simplicity can inspire our body, humility can inspire our vital, sincerity can inspire our mind and purity can inspire our heart to have peace in the outer world.

In the inner world,
Sleeplessly
If you can multiply peace-light,
Then in the outer world,
Unconditionally
You can multiply
Love-delight.

Peace begins when we come to realise that the world does not need our guidance.

What is peace? Peace is our liberation from bondage. What is liberation? Liberation is our universal oneness with God the Unity and God the Multiplicity. What is bondage? Bondage is the dance of our unlit ego. What is ego? Ego is the unreal in us. And what is the real in us? The real in us is Truth; the real in us is God. God and Truth are inseparable, the obverse and reverse of the same coin.

Why are you moving
From one country to another
To find peace?
The sea of peace
Is just inside
Your mind's silence-sky.

When you feel peace in infinite measure, the question of insecurity does not arise.

If we want to achieve peace in our inner and outer life, then we must know the necessity of reciprocal inclusiveness and not mutual exclusiveness. Earth and Heaven must be united. Heaven has the silence of the soul. Earth has the sound of life. The silence of the soul leads us to our Source, the highest Reality; and the sound of life allows us to manifest what is within that highest Reality. In the inclusiveness of earth and Heaven we can achieve peace.

> *Be conscious of your outer strength.*
> *You will be divinely powerful.*
> *Be conscious of your inner strength.*
> *You will be supremely peaceful.*

Peace is the inner man's inner goodness. Peace is the outer man's outer greatness.

The ancient dream of cooperation is not a human dream which has very little to do with reality. The ancient dream, to be precise, is not a dream at all but a faultless and divine vision—an unhorizoned vision—which is slowly, steadily and unerringly shaping the individual and collective destiny in humanity's march towards the supreme goal of universal oneness and transcendental newness. The world is evolving and progressing and reaching a higher standard of life. It is not moving in a horizontal way, but in a spiral. Therefore, at times this progress is not immediately noticeable. At times it confuses and baffles our human mind. But on the strength of our inner oneness with the world situation and world evolution, we see unmistakably the world's slow and steady progress.

To lessen world tension
Each seeker-heart must feed
The peace-starving humanity.

When the age of reason ends, the heart of peace will inundate the entire world.

Peace is the most effective weapon with which to conquer injustice. When you pray and meditate, your whole being becomes flooded with peace. Then, no matter what other people do, you will just feel that they are your own children playing in front of you. You will say, "These are all children. What more can I expect from them?" But right now, you become angry and upset instead. If you pray and meditate regularly, you will soon feel that your peace is infinitely stronger, more fulfilling and more energizing than the unfortunate situations that others may create.

Since you are walking
The peace-path,
Your mind will totally forget
That once upon a time
It was overcrowded with dark thoughts.

Peace is life. Peace is bliss eternal.

Worries—mental, vital and physical—do exist. But it is up to us whether to accept them or reject them. To be sure, they are not inevitable facts of life. Since our Almighty Father is all peace, our common heritage is peace. It is a Himalayan blunder to widen the broadway of future repentance by misusing and neglecting the golden opportunities that are presented to us. We must resolve here and now, amidst all our daily activities, to throw ourselves, heart and soul, into the sea of peace.

My soul asks my heart
Every day
To take some peace-light
From my soul
And give it to my peaceless mind.

Only a heart of peace can enjoy the supreme Friendship of God.

The seeker in a human being will never be satisfied unless and until the world problems are solved. The real seeker in us knows that there is a way to solve all the countless problems of the world, and that way is to accept the world problems as such and then try to bring perfection into the world problems. How do we accept the world problems? We accept the world problems as our own problems, personal problems. And how do we perfect the world problems? We perfect the world problems by perfecting ourselves and by perfecting the things that we claim as our own.

Peace I feel
In infinite measure
When my life becomes
The fragrance
Of my gratitude-heart.

June

Love

There is only one thing that was, is and forever shall be, and that is love: the love that created, the love that nourishes, the love that sustains God's universe.

Peace is the child of divine Love and at the same time love is the child of peace. If we pray to God or meditate on God in our vital life, then when divine Love descends from above, our emotional life is purified. When our emotional life is purified, at that time we become peaceful. Then love gives birth to peace; love is the mother. But when we meditate in the physical world, that is to say in our gross physical body which can be restless, aggressive or lethargic, we try to bring down peace from above. When peace descends, we get a kind of satisfaction or joy. And that joy we try to transfer to others in the form of love. Love that is founded upon peace is naturally the child of peace.

I long to live
Only at one place,
And that place is
Where love eternally rules.

JUNE 2

I know how to love just because I am God's alone.

If you want to express and manifest divine Love in the physical world, you have to use your spiritual will-power. This will-power is not aggressive; it is all surrender. On the strength of your conscious oneness with the Supreme's Will, you will be able to bring forward your spiritual will- power. When it is sanctioned by the Supreme, automatically and spontaneously you will have a way to use your divine will-power to express love for humanity. When you really possess this divine will-power, then even in your unconscious movements your pure love will radiate. Those around you will undoubtedly feel the divine love and get the utmost benefit from your divine presence.

My first mistake was
I did not love God
Unconditionally.
My last mistake was
I did not rectify
My first mistake.

JUNE 3

Love the world with the feeling that the world is God. You will revive the truth.

You can express and manifest love in the physical world through your pure meditation. When you are in your deepest meditation, try to feel your purest love. Then think of the person that you love. By concentrating on him you can inject your pure divine Love into him. By looking at a person with the eyes of your soul, you can manifest love in the physical world.

To love those who love us
Is to do the right thing.
To love those who do not love us
Is to do the nice thing.
To love God who always loves us
Is to do the wise thing.
When we do the right thing, we are free.
When we do the nice thing, we are safe.
When we do the wise thing, we are fulfilled.

Love your family much. This is your great duty. Love mankind more. This is your greater duty. Love God most. This is your greatest duty, the Duty Supreme.

If love means to possess someone or something, then that is not real love, not pure love. If love means to give oneself, to become one with everything and with humanity, then that is real love. Real love is total oneness with the object loved and with the Possessor of love. Who is the Possessor of love? God. Without love, we cannot become one with God. Love is the inner bond, the inner connection, the inner link between man and God. We must always approach God through love.

Do not try to go near God with fear.
You will see that He is not approachable.
Go to God with your love.
You will see that He is not only approachable
But always available.

He who loves never grows old. God is a shining example.

If you really want to love humanity, then you have to love humanity as it stands now and not expect it to come to a specific standard. If humanity had to become perfect before it could be accepted by you, then it would not need your love, affection and concern. But right now, in its imperfect state of consciousness, humanity does need your love. Give humanity unreservedly even the most insignificant and limited love that you have at your disposal. This is the golden opportunity. Once you miss this opportunity, your future suffering will be beyond your endurance, because a day will come when you will realise that humanity's imperfection is your own imperfection.

My heart's love-boat
Has room even for those
Who are suffering
From jealousy-monster.

God the Master becomes God the Slave the moment we soulfully love Him.

Love is the secret key to open God's Door. We must always approach God through love. The first step is love; the second step is devotion; the third step is surrender. First we have to love God; then we have to devote ourselves to Him alone; finally we have to be at His Feet and fulfil ourselves. So if we go through our life's journey with absolute love, we can never fail to reach God or fulfil Him in our own lives or in humanity. Where there is pure love, divine Love, there is fulfilment. Where there is no divine Love, it is all misery, frustration and, ultimately, spiritual death.

Do you want to discover God?
Then embark
On your love-expedition.

Love has another name: sacrifice. When sacrifice is pure, love is sure. When love is divine, in sacrifice there can be no "mine," no "thine."

Selfless love is when we love and does not care for anything in return; we become one with the object of our adoration. In this love there is a subtle feeling that the Beloved will give us the best fruit because we will not bother Him with silly emotional problems or desires, with "Give me this," or "Give me that." In selfless love, that stage has been done away with. The seeker knows that the Supreme will give him something nice, something worth possessing; he has not to ask for anything. This is selfless love.

You do not have to prove
God's Love for you.
Just feel that you live
Only for God's Love.

Love is the secret of oneness. Sacrifice is the strength of oneness.

Every day the Almighty Father, the ever-compassionate Father, gives us ample opportunity to discover something new. The thing that we are discovering is love, Love divine. Love divine is at once eternally ancient and eternally new. When we discover Love divine within us, we grow into the very image of God the eternal Lover and God the eternal Beloved, who ever abides within us.

My Lord Supreme,
I have not realised You,
I may not realise You
In this lifetime.
But will You not do me
A big favour?
Will You not give me the capacity
To love You,
Only love You, only love You?

My meditation invites God, the supreme Guest. My love serves and feeds God, the eternal Beloved.

If we practise what we preach, then wisdom becomes our profession. What we practise and what we preach should be the same: love. We tell the world to love, but we may not actually offer love to the world. But if we offer love and become love, then we can most assuredly expect to see love in the world at large. It is God's Love-Power that compels us to think of Him, to pray to Him, to meditate on Him and to claim Him as our very own. As God claims us as His very own on the strength of His own Love-Power, so also He tells us and inspires us and begs us to claim Him as our very own on the strength of our love for Him.

My love-deposits
In God's Heart-Bank
Give God infinite Delight.

JUNE 10

Divine Love is the running stream and the unceasing source of nectar.

Try to cultivate divine Love. Try to love humanity soulfully. You may say, "How can I love others when I do not know how to love myself?" I will tell you how you can love yourself. You can love yourself most successfully just by loving God unreservedly. You may ask, "How can I love God when I do not know what love is?" I will tell you what love is. Love is the transforming power in our human nature. Love transforms our life of stark bondage into the life of mightiest freedom. Love cries for life. Love fights for life. And, finally love grows into the Life Eternal.

The first and the last step
Must be taken
Soulfully and sleeplessly:
I love God.
I love God unconditionally.

God loved you, loves you and will always love you. But you will feel His Love infinitely more than you feel it now if you can soulfully say only once that you are of Him and for Him alone.

Why should God love me? God loves me because I love mankind. There is another reason, too. God loves me because I love His entire Creation. I know and feel that God can never be separated from His Creation. Creator and Creation are one, inseparable. When we appreciate the Creation, the Creator is pleased and satisfied. When we ourselves create something, produce something, build something, people notice our achievement and appreciate it deeply. We are pleased because it is we who have done it. Similarly, the universe is God's Creation. When we love the universe, we simultaneously love God the Creator and God the Creation; and both the Creator and the Creation will be pleased with us.

Love,
Love the world.
Otherwise, you will be forced
To carry the heaviest load:
Your own bitter self.

When I love only God unconditionally, endless is my satisfaction-delight. When I love only myself sleeplessly, endless is my frustration-destruction.

Because I love God, Truth loves me. Truth has no existence without God. God is the very breath of Truth. Truth and God are one, indivisible. On the one hand, Truth is another name for God. On the other hand, Truth cannot exist without God, whereas God can at each moment transcend Truth—earthly truth and Heavenly Truth, earth-bound truth and Heavenward Truth. Even His own Transcendental Truth God can transcend at His own sweet Will. Inside God is the existence of Truth. In our very appreciation of God, Truth is fed and nourished. And Truth rightly feels that its unique message to the world can be spread only when we truly love its Possessor, God.

Surrendered love
Multiplied by gratitude-life
Equals God's supreme Satisfaction.

The love of the Supreme is my life.

Because I love the truth, I love myself. A human being is the expression of truth. He is not the expression of ignorance, falsehood, darkness and death. No, he is the embodiment, realisation and expression of truth—the lesser truth, the higher truth and the highest Truth. Each moment the divine truth is transcending its boundaries in us. We see it, feel it and realise it when we live the inner life, the life of the soul. Because I love the truth, I really and truly love myself. My existence and truth are the obverse and the reverse of the same coin, which is the inner being or soul, the representative of the Supreme here on earth.

How will you recognize Heaven?
You will recognize Heaven
With your unconditional oneness-love
For the world.

God's supreme Love manifests in me and through me to transform my human problems into my divine opportunities.

I love myself. What do I love about myself? If I love my body for the sake of my body, tomorrow I shall be frustrated because there are millions of human beings on earth who are more beautiful than I am. If I love my mind for the sake of my mind, tomorrow I shall see millions of mental giants right in front of me, and my mental capacity will fade into insignificance. If I love my vital dynamism for the sake of my vital dynamism, then I shall see that there are millions of people who are inundated with striking dynamism. Similarly, if I love anything else of my own, for its own sake, I am bound to be frustrated. But if I love myself just because God is expressing Himself through this body, vital, mind and heart, then I see that I am unique and peerless in the whole history of the universe.

Every day
Your God-love is accelerating.
That means
Every day God is making
An infinitely more significant Promise
In and through you to mankind.

JUNE 15

We need love to feel the Beloved within and the Lover without.

Each individual can love himself just because he is a direct channel of the Divine. God wants to express Himself in each individual in a unique way. When we become consciously and fully one with God, we not only fulfil Him but we also fulfil ourselves. When I say that I really and truly love myself because I love truth, it means that I consciously feel that truth is constantly breathing in me, with me and for me.

In your heart-garden
There are many love-plants.
Can you not give away
Some of these plants
To truth-seekers and God-lovers?

Love radiates the life of harmony, brightens the joy of consciousness and sharpens the sword of intuition.

My very breath on earth is the living reality of truth. I love and adore myself at every moment—not because of my sound body, dynamic vital, refined mind and pure heart, but because God is inside me, God is utilising me, God is fulfilling Himself in me and through me. This is the sole reason why my body, vital, mind and heart are loved by me and must be loved by me. Each individual has to be surcharged with this supreme Truth. He should consciously feel that his life on earth is the outer manifestation of the Supreme's inner Breath.

A moment's truth
Can and shall make the world beautiful.
A moment's peace
Can and shall save the world.
A moment's love
Can and shall make the world perfect.

Human love is an express train: destination—frustration. Divine Love is a local train: destination—illumination.

When we follow the path of love, we find our spiritual life, our inner life, most satisfactory. Here God is dearest to us, not because He is Omnipotent, Omnipresent or Omniscient, but because He is all Love. God, our Eternal Father, can be approached most successfully and in a way that seems most convincing, through love. When we approach Him through love, we see that He is all Love; and when we just open our eyes and try to look at Him, we see that He is right in front of us, blessing us, embracing us. He says, "My child, I have been all the time waiting for you." Here love means one's constant feeling of inseparable oneness with one's Beloved.

When I inundate my life
With love,
I see deep inside me
The congress of giant souls.

Red-angered eyes say: "Whether thou lovest me or not, I have come to kill thee." But soul-illumined eyes say: "I see God in thee and love thee whether thou killest me or not."

When we love God, our problem is over. True, we all do not see God face to face. But we can imagine for a fleeting second that God with all His Love abides in our dear and near ones. Let us try to see the face of our Beloved in our dear ones. Where there is love, true love, there is all oneness.

Love I always must.
When I love mankind,
I am the subject of constant admiration
In the outer world.
When I love God,
I am the subject of constant admiration
In the inner world.

To have no love for others is in no way a step towards God-realisation. On the contrary, fellow-feeling helps one considerably to live in the Divine Consciousness.

Devotion is the intensity in love, and surrender is the fulfilment of love. Why do we love? We love because at every moment we are pinched with hunger to realise the highest, to feel the inmost, to be consciously one with the universe, with the universal truth, light, peace and bliss, and to be completely fulfilled. How to love? If we love with a view to achieving something from others, then our love is no love. Love means constant self-offering on the strength of our own inner aspiration.

Do you want
To deserve God's Love?
Then serve God the man
In God's unfinished Creation.

It is not enough to love God in the God-lover. We must also love God in the God-hater.

Our conception of God is so peculiar. We feel that God is like a primary school teacher, who is ready to beat us black and blue if we deviate an inch from the path of truth. But that conception of God is absurd. There is no such being as God the tyrant. There is only one God, and that God is God the Love. This God does not punish us. This God is constantly shaping us in His own Way. It is He who is the Doer, it is He who is the Action and it is He who is the Enjoyer, both in the action and in the result. But we feel that we are the doers, and that if we do something wrong God will punish us mercilessly. But this is not so. It is God's Drama that each individual embodies. It is God's Reality that each individual has to manifest here on earth. It is in each human being that God's Reality lives.

If somebody asks you for your kindness,
Do you know what you give
To that person actually?
You give him
Your extraordinary love-power.

God has given me the love needed to love the world.

You can increase your capacity to accept love by giving love to others. The more you give, the more you receive. So if you are able to give more love to mankind, then you will be able to receive from mankind. You can spread your love to people provided you can see all the time your Beloved inside them. Your Beloved is the Supreme. If you see the Supreme inside them, then you will do everything for them. If you see beauty inside something, then you will touch it. If you do not see beauty, if you see darkness and ugliness, you will not touch it. So if you see God's Presence inside humanity, then only will you love humanity. If you can see the Beloved Supreme inside each and every human being, then automatically you will have love and respect for humanity.

The only effective way
To love man
Is to first love God
Sleeplessly.

To love only your own religion is to love the body-reality of sound-division. To love all re-ligions equally is to love the soul-immortality of silence-oneness.

God the Love is inside everything that we see. If we love God, and we do love Him because He is all Love, then whatever He has created, we also love. He is bound to be in His Creation just because He is everywhere, just because He is omnipresent. So if you can love God the Love, then automatically you increase your love for everything. God the Love embraces everything and is inside everything. So if you care for the Source, the Creator, then automatically you care for the Creation.

It is beneath the dignity
Of a loving heart
To wear any disguise.

Human love is often the terrible attraction of bodies and nerves; divine Love is the ever-blossoming affinity of souls.

You can have heartfelt love for all humanity only when you love the Source. God created us. We did not create God. So in order to love all humanity, you have to go to humanity's source, God. If you love the root, then only can you love the tree. The root here is God. If you are conscious of the Source and the qualities the Source has, then only can you really love mankind. You cannot love any human being unless and until you love God. If you can make yourself feel that you love God and God alone, and nobody else, then you love everyone, for God is Someone who is inside everyone.

Life
Can be stronger
Than death
If man learns
Carefully and unmistakably
The language of love.

Pure love and untold misery cannot live together. Pure love is the body's constant oneness with the soul's flood of delight.

If I feel that God really loves me, then only can I have true and abiding happiness. The Creator is all love for His creation. But the Creation quite often does not feel it or realise it. Since I am part of God's Creation, it is my bounden duty to feel God's Love at every moment. Only then will I try to become good, divine and perfect, and try to please Him in His own Way.

The person with the ultimate power
Knows that without love
His life is dry and dust-filled.

**How to overcome destructive criticism? Just love a
little more. That is all.**

You can be more receptive to the divine Love if you
can feel every day that your Source is all Love, and
that you are on earth to offer constantly, in thought
and in action, the love that you already have. At every
moment you have many thoughts, so you can offer
love through each of your thoughts. And each time
you do something, you can feel that this action is
nothing but an expression of love. Right now, offering love through thought and action is of supreme
importance in your life. While thinking and while
acting, if you can feel that you are offering love to
mankind, to the rest of the world, then you can be
more receptive to the universal love. In this way you
can feel that God's divine Love is all for you.

*If you want to work
In an aura of love,
Then invite your soul
Every morning
To enlighten your mind.*

Love conquers all that is unlike God. It is, indeed, supreme over all.

If we have peace, then only we can love. When a mother has peace of mind, then she loves her child. If she has no peace of mind, then she strikes the child right and left. Where is love at that time? She will tell the child, "It is for your good that I am doing this." But no, it is only her lack of wisdom, her own undivine nature that is compelling her to strike the child. If the mother has peace in boundless measure, then naturally she will be a continuous and constant expression of love for her children.

> *Which master do you want?*
> *The doubting mind.*
> *Which master do you need?*
> *The loving heart.*

Love is the only law.

We love God because we feel that He is all Love. Just because we love God, we feel that it is our bounden duty to devote ourselves to Him and please Him. But we see that our love and service are not enough; surrender is also necessary. If we do not surrender our individual will to His Will, we will make many mistakes when we try to love Him and serve Him in our own unillumined way. But if we surrender to His Will, then we shall love Him in the way He has chosen for us, which is the right way.

> *To see*
> *A face of love*
> *Is to feel*
> *A heart of peace.*

Because of your constant and unconditional love for God, nobody can inspire you to do anything wrong.

I prayed to God for power. He said, "Take it and use it." I prayed to God for light. He said, "Take it and spread it." I prayed to God for peace. He said, "Take it and unveil your divinity." I prayed to God for bliss. He said, "Take it and stay in your Source." I prayed to God for love. He said, "Take Me; I am yours."

My mind thinks
God is beautiful
Because
My heart loves God.

My heart knows
God is beautiful
Because
My soul loves God.

Love of God is the seeker's greatest opportunity to realise God.

The heart flies precisely because it loves. What does it love? It loves oneness—oneness within, oneness without, oneness with the Inner Pilot, its Beloved Supreme. Just because it loves oneness, and just because it loves the Beloved Supreme constantly, unreservedly and unconditionally, it is able to fly at every moment in the firmament of all-illumining Consciousness.

My heart tells my mind,
"O my searching mind,
Do not be satisfied
With your present achievement.
You want to love the Inner Pilot most,
But that is not enough.
You have to love
The Inner Pilot only."

When the power of love replaces the love of power, man will have a new name: God.

When we come face to face with God, He asks us to offer Him what we have. If we can offer Him our real treasure, a heart of love, He immediately accepts it and says, "You have passed your examination." But if we offer God all our world-possessions, physical, vital, mental possessions—but do not bring Him love, then He will not be satisfied. God will say, "No, bring Me your heart of love; that is your true treasure. And once I have your true treasure, then I will give you My Treasure, which is Light and Delight in infinite measure."

If you are a genuine God-lover,
Then at every moment
Be prepared
For the coming God-Hour.

July

Light

JULY 1

Light is the real food to eat.

Of all the divine qualities, unfortunately light is wanted least, even though it is needed most by all. People want peace, joy and power, but very rarely do they want light. Unconsciously or consciously they are afraid of light. They feel that the effulgence of light will uproot the ignorance-tree which they embody. They feel that the divine light will expose their imperfections, limitations and bondage. This is not true. The divine light embraces the world in all its ignorance. Something more, the divine light feels that it is its bounden duty to elevate the human consciousness into the plenitude of the Life Divine.

If you are a seeker
Of silence-light,
Then God will grant you
An eternal dawn
In His universal Heart.

Light is the life of the inner world.

When we have the inner experience of light, we realise that the finite can embody and reveal the Infinite and, at the same time, the Infinite can manifest its Infinity, Eternity and Immortality in and through the finite. When we have the inner experience of light, we feel the constant necessity of knowing whether we are working for God, whether we are constantly taking God's side or whether God is taking our side. After we have had the inner experience of light, we always want to take God's side. We do not want and do not allow God to take our side. This is the experience that transcends all other experiences. When one has had the full inner experience of infinite Light, one always takes the side of the Supreme.

If you do not curtail
Your earthly roamings,
You will not be able to launch
The ship of perfection-light.

On earth nothing is more beautiful than God's Patience-Light.

You want to see the light. Either you are trying to enter into the vastness of this light or you are trying to bring to the fore the light that you already have. Wonderful! But there are many people who are afraid of light. They say, "Yes, we want light." But the moment light comes to them, they feel that they are going to be exposed. People feel that if they can hide themselves in a dark room, then they will be in a position to see the world and pass judgement, but that nobody will be able to see them. This is their hope. So their darkness, they feel, is a kind of safety and security. When light comes and is ready to enter into them, they feel that all their weaknesses and limitations, all their negative ideas and negative thoughts, will be exposed. But the very function of light is to illumine, not to expose; to transform our negative and destructive thoughts into positive and affirmative thoughts.

Time will crumble soon
If you do not start living
For God's Satisfaction-Light
Inside your heart's aspiration-height.

In Heaven nothing is more beautiful than God's Compassion-Light.

You want to know how you can receive light or how you can bring light to the fore. For that you need preparation, and what is that preparation? The preparation is your pure concentration, your pure meditation. When you start your meditation or concentration, try to feel that you have come from light and you are inside light. This is not your imagination; this is not your mental hallucination. Far from it! It is a real, solid, concrete truth that you embody light and that you are light itself. You will see that there is a spontaneous flow of light from within. First you will feel it inside your heart. Then you will feel it in your forehead, in the third eye; and finally you will feel it all over.

Darkness is light:
This is what my mind thinks.
Light is delight:
This what my heart feels.

In me nothing is more beautiful than God's Forgiveness-Light.

There is another way of seeing light. While breathing, when you draw in the breath, please feel that you are breathing in something that is purifying all that has to be purified inside you and, at the same time, energising all that is unfed. In the beginning, there are quite a few things inside you that have to be purified. There are quite a few things which are hungry. So when you feel that you are feeding, energising and, at the same time, purifying, then you will see that light becomes absolutely natural.

He was faithful
To God's Compassion-Light.
Therefore
God made his life
Supremely beautiful.

JULY 6

When light enters into our physical con-sciousness, every kind of fear is bound to disappear.

In the spiritual life we want God, but as soon as we see a little of His infinite Light, we are scared to death. We feel that all our imperfections will be exposed. Instead, always we have to feel that God's Light is there only to illumine us. There is no limit to our achievement, no limit to our realisation, no limit to our God-manifestation, because the light within us will constantly be guiding us. So we do not have to be afraid of anything.

Seeing the heart
Flooded with the soul's light,
The mind cursed itself:
"Oh, why am I so stupid!
Why do I not visit my soul
Every day?"

When we pray and meditate, we receive light and everything is clear to us.

Sometimes the aspirant will only be able to imagine God, and sometimes, in spite of his outer efforts, he may not feel the presence of God in himself, and sometimes he may even forget the existence of God. But he has to bear in mind that he has a Source and that Source is Light, boundless Light, infinite Light. He has been wallowing in the pleasures of ignorance for many years and he has not yet come out of ignorance. But he has to feel that his Source is not ignorance; his Source is Light and Delight. He is for that Source and he is making a conscious effort to return to his Source. While returning, he is manifesting God-Delight here on earth. If he can remember this, then he will feel a constant sense of satisfaction in his life. He will feel light, more light, abundant light, infinite Light in his outer and inner life.

His heart is crying
To hear
The voice of silence-light.
His soul is crying
To become
God's Satisfaction-Delight.

JULY 8

The outer experience of light is the trans-formation of binding desires into liberating freedom. The inner experience of Light is the transformation of earth's fate into God's Face.

To meditate on a quality, let us say light, first try to imagine what will happen when that quality enters into you. Try to imagine what will happen if light enters into you. The answer is that illumination will take place. Put illumination in front of your mental vision and feel that slowly, steadily and unerringly you are growing into illumination itself. In this way, imagination will give you the message of reality. Then you have to feel that this reality is nothing other than your true self, and that you have to grow into this reality.

> *No matter how fleeting*
> *Your smile is,*
> *Your smile is the very beginning*
> *Of your wisdom-light.*

When one wants to expand oneself inwardly, the light that is there is bound to guide and illumine him.

The mind needs a superior power to keep it quiet. This superior power is the power of the soul. We have to bring to the fore the light of the soul, which has unlimited power. In the outer world, when somebody is superior in strength or power, he tries to punish the inferior. But in the spiritual world, the light of the soul will not torture or punish the mind. On the contrary, it will act like a most affectionate mother who feels that the imperfections of her child are her own imperfections. The heart will feel the obscurity, impurity and darkness of the mind as its own imperfections and, at the same time, the heart will be in a position to offer its light to the mind. In pin-drop silence it will try to transform the nature of the mind.

Do not wait inactively
For progress-light,
Or you will always remain
A deplorable failure.

The dance of light awakens the wings of life to soar into the Silence of the Absolute Supreme.

The source of the higher light is actually the soul. The moment we can have free access to our inner being or to the soul, we will see that this light is coming to the fore to permeate our whole outer existence.

Say "No"
When you have to;
Say "Yes"
When you want to.
This is how you can succeed
In your world of self-dedication.
This is how you can proceed
In your world of self-illumination.

The purest, highest light is the Light of the Absolute Supreme.

The Light of the Supreme can be seen and, at the same time, it can be felt or experienced. When we have established our constant, eternal and inseparable oneness with the Highest, the experience that we get is purest light. If we have to define the purest light, we can say that it is nothing but an experience of the Supreme in the Supreme. When we consciously feel our permanent and complete oneness with the Absolute Supreme, we get an eternal and everlasting experience of real, purest light, and the purest consciousness of the Supreme is put at our disposal.

In silence-light
The soul is playing
Its own divine music
For the total transformation
Of the body, vital, mind and heart.

We need light to see the Creator within and the Creation without.

We achieve the experience of purest light on the strength of our inner cry. If we work outwardly for material wealth or power, eventually we achieve these outer things. When we want to do something or achieve something, we have to work for it. Right now our goal is purest light. In this case, our work is to cry inwardly. We have to inwardly cry like a child for inseparable oneness with the Supreme. The child cries for what it wants, and the mother always comes. No matter where she is, she comes to offer the child whatever it wants. Similarly, when we cry in the inmost recesses of our heart, our request is granted. But everything depends on the sincerity of our inner cry. If our cry is sincere, God is bound to grant it. If we cry inwardly for spiritual things—for peace, light, bliss—then we are bound to achieve these divine qualities.

Feed your mind with your soul's
Illumination-light-food.
You will be the happiest person
In God's entire Creation.

When a man lives and swims in the sea of his soul's light, he is all gratitude. He is the constant expression and spontaneous revelation of God the Receiver and God the Achiever.

Light is the power of the Supreme that illumines and transforms ignorance. Light is the capacity of the Supreme that transforms darkness into illumination-light. Anything that transforms our existence is light. Light, you can say, is the life-breath of the Supreme. Each colour has a special meaning. Blue light is Infinity, vastness; white light is purity. Green light is freshness, life-energy, new life. Like that, each colour has a significance.

I no more see the trouble-bridge
On my life's turbulent river,
For God has built a bridge
With His Compassion-Light.

When the mind and death are transcended, man will have a new home: Light, the Light of the Beyond.

When you meditate, light is operating in and through you. The light which you get during your meditation is not only for your use but for others' use as well. When you receive light, if you feel that you can use it at your sweet will, this is the wrong attitude. God gives us light and He uses this light in and through us for others. It is true that sometimes we misuse light. We misuse light when we want to possess the world for our own sake. But if we want to accept the world for God's sake, then we will never misuse light. If we really want to accept the world for God's use, then at that time we do not try to possess the world. Consciously we jump into the sea of silence and activity. God gives us the opportunity or God Himself acts as the opportunity in the form of light so that we can enter into the wide world. At that time, we do not possess anything; we just exercise our feeling of oneness.

God now is Light,
Delight, Delight,
My All, my All.
God now is Light.

The outer experience of light is immediate inspiration. The inner experience of light is eternal aspiration.

If it is real light, if it is pure, divine light, then rest assured that your mind cannot doubt what you are seeing. The mind does not have the capacity to doubt divine light while you are seeing it. If you are doubting it while seeing it, that means it is not the real light that you are seeing. The effulgence of light is such that it will not allow any suspicion or doubt to enter in. You cannot doubt while seeing light if it is absolutely the purest light of the divine Consciousness. When the real light, divine light, supreme light appears, at that time the mind is obliterated; it does not function at all. The mind cannot exist when the divine light comes. The entire being becomes all soul, all heart, all oneness.

If your life is not surcharged
With God's Compassion-Light,
Then your life will be poisoned
By ignorance-breath.

JULY 16

The very function of spiritual light is to illumine and transform our darkness. Spiritual light, inner light, illumines our age-long imperfections and bondage.

The mind does have the capacity to doubt divine light afterwards. First you see the light and at that time the mind is divine. Then, after twelve hours or even five minutes, the mind will gather strength and try to throw suspicion into your experience of light. When your consciousness descends, when the light goes away from your physical awareness, at that time you can doubt the light that you saw. If right now God stands before you, you are not going to doubt Him. But the moment God disappears from your outer vision, you can doubt God.

If you can penetrate your mind
With your soul's transcendental light,
Then you will be able to answer
The universal question easily:
"Who am I?"

When we see the divine light, we feel happy. When we feel the divine light, we become strong. And when we grow into the divine light, our life becomes fruitful.

Because of your oneness with your body you do not doubt your eyes, you do not doubt your nose. You know that you are part and parcel of your body and that your body is part and parcel of your life; so you do not doubt. Similarly, divine light is your real existence. How can you deny or doubt your own existence? But after the experience is over, when you do not feel the light as your own, at that time the mind may throw suspicion and doubt into you.

In the world of light
I fly from peak to peak.
Indeed, this is my perfection-progress.

In the world of night
I stumble from frustration-window
To destruction-door.
Indeed, this is my achievement-experience.

When we cry to see the transcendental Light and when we try to perfect our outer nature, our perfection does not remain a far cry.

"Do not push, do not pull." We accept our life as it is; then we try to transform it. But we do not do it by hook or by crook. The divine means is through aspiration. If we pull beyond our capacity, we will break. If a child wants to carry something very heavy, beyond his capacity, he will suffer. Slow and steady wins the race. Here capacity is receptivity. If we develop great receptivity, then no matter how high our spiritual height or how much we bring down from above, we will be able to assimilate it. If the container is very large, we do not have to worry. So when we aspire to climb up to the highest height, we have to aspire for expansion. Not only beginners, but also highly developed seekers have suffered from deplorable experiences. The physical isn't large enough to hold the peace, light and power that the psychic brings down. So there should be a perfect harmony between the physical capacity and the heart's capacity.

Love is life.
Life is light.
Light is God's Meditation and man's salvation.

In order to enter into the invisible universe, what we need is the soul's illumining light.

If we really want the inner light, if we really have the inner cry to see God face to face, there can be nothing either on earth or in Heaven to deny us, to deny our soul's inmost quest. Each individual being has limited freedom. This freedom can be utilised either to aspire or to desire. If we desire, the teeming clouds will undoubtedly eclipse our knowledge-sun. If we aspire, God, the Inner Pilot, will inspire us to run fast, faster, fastest towards the Destined Goal, the Goal of the Beyond.

> O Bird of Light, O Bird of Light,
> With your glowing and flowing flames
> Do enter into my heart once again.
> You are calling me to climb up
> And fly into the blue.
> But how can I?
> My heart is in prison,
> In the strangled breath of a tiny room.
> O Bird of Light, O Bird of Light,
> O Bird of Light Supreme.
> I me, I pray, keep not an iota of gloom.

To illumine our life we need pure thoughts. Each pure thought is more precious than all the diamonds of the world, for God's Breath abides only in man's pure thoughts.

It is in our inner existence that we can grow into an adamantine will; and when we use our adamantine will, which we can easily have at our behest, we can conquer the very breath of fear. Here on earth our inner adamantine and indomitable will can and will reign supreme. Only one thing we need: a conscious awareness of the divine light which is ours. It is our birthright to realise and fulfil this inner light.

The moments of God's Justice-Light
Are brief, very brief.

The days of God's Compassion-Height
Are long, very long.

Without light, nothing can be accomplished in the spiritual life. With light, everything can be accomplished. In light, everything is already accomplished.

There can be no fear, there cannot be even an iota of fear when we live in the effulgence of our soul. To live constantly in the divine effulgence of our soul only one thing is needed: a conscious inner cry. This inner cry is called aspiration, the mounting flame deep within us. When this flame rises up towards the highest, it illumines everything around it. Darkness is transformed into light, fear into strength, doubt into certainty, ignorance into wisdom and death into Immortality.

How to conquer fear?
With oneness within
And oneness without.
In oneness-light
There can be no fear.

Light makes us feel that we are everything, that we can do everything, that we can become everything.

Some people cry for light sincerely, but without satisfactory results, simply because God's destined Hour has not yet arrived. If a farmer feels that on the very day that he starts working very hard to cultivate his land he should get a bumper crop he will get disgusted and abandon the field when he sees no results after a few weeks of sincere effort. But although sincerity is important, time is still a great factor. The field can only produce satisfactory fruit at God's own time. If we are one hundred percent surrendered, we will feel that if we are not getting the satisfactory results, we will wait forever for God's Hour.

God gave me the heart of light
To live,
To cry
And succeed.

God gave me the light of heart
To be,
To smile
And proceed.

Since you have the strongest desire to be invit-ed by God, then breathe in by far the greatest prayer: patience-light.

What we sincerely need is light. But if light does not come, we must be ready to wait for Eternity for infinite Light to surcharge our inner and outer being. Falsehood will immediately feel that we are ready to wait for millions of years in order to bathe in the sea of light, and it will lose its interest in us. If God wants to, He can give us what we want at once, but if He feels that this is not the appropriate time, we have to wait. Then if we have patience, which itself is the extension of light or of consciousness, we can feel that we are increasing the light that we have and the light that is entering into us.

Patience-light
Is the sleepless breath
Of my self-giving heart
For my Beloved Supreme.

Our love of Consciousness-Light can and will expedite our achievement in the body.

The first thing we have to do in our life is pray and meditate. Early in the morning, if we pray to God, we enter into the world of the Source. Then we try to offer the light that we have received from our prayer and meditation to the world around us. First we achieve and then we give. If I do not have any light, then what am I going to give?

Morning is the time
To accept God's Love-Light.

Noon is the time
To become God's Love-Height.

Evening is the time
To radiate God's Love-Delight.

Our devotion to the Consciousness-Light can and will expedite our achievement in the vital.

Let us have infinite patience and boundless courage in our quest for the inner light. And if light does not come, let us not compromise at all with darkness and falsehood. We must be prepared to sacrifice our life for our goal of divine light. Then truth will win the battle against falsehood permanently.

To disarm death
The human heart must pray
To God's Compassion
Sleeplessly,
And the human life must surrender
To God's Light
Unconditionally.

Our surrender to the Consciousness-Light can and will expedite our achievement in the mind.

When you have done something wrong, consider that it is over. "The past is dust" is my philosophy. Let us avail ourselves of today's golden opportunity to do the right thing. Let us build our foundation on a solid rock. Let us grow from light to more light, to abundant light, to infinite Light. Light is our Source, and from light we can grow. But if we feed on the darkness of negativity we will not be able to grow at all.

Unless you are prepared
To cheerfully accept
God's Justice-Light,
How can you please God?

Our constant and inseparable oneness with the Consciousness-Light can and will expedite our achievement in the heart.

One can become more competent in fulfilling one's earthly duties by first doing one's Heavenly duties. Heavenly duties will never ask you to neglect your earthly duties. Only you have to do the first things first. Your Heavenly duty is to remain in light. If you are inundated with light, then only can you enter into darkness and do what is needed there. Earthly duties are full of darkness. Heavenly duties are prayer, concentration, meditation, contemplation. If you do your Heavenly duties first, you eventually embody light. Then, with this light, you can enter into the earthly duties. So first things first. With your Heavenly duties—prayer, meditation, concentration— you will invoke light; and once you are surcharged with light, then you will attend to the earthly duties. Otherwise, you will never be able to acquire enough capacity to discharge your earthly duties.

If you do not fulfil
Your outer obligations,
Your inner illumination
Will always remain a far cry.

Illumination encompasses the destruction-world, the possession-world and the temptation-world.

Outer compassion comes from inner illumination. If one is inwardly illumined, then automatically his illumination will take the form of compassion in the outer life. First comes inner illumination; then comes the manifestation of this inner illumination in the outer life. This is compassion. If one says that he is offering compassion before he is inwardly illumined, he is only deceiving himself. What he calls compassion is only his unconscious way of showing attachment towards the earth-consciousness.

He who has wisdom,
Light and delight
Will never be caught
In the world's unhappiness-net.

We should always try to aim at illumination to save our earth-bound life from the destruction-world, and to transform our earth-bound life into the Heaven-free world.

Outer light is knowledge; inner light is realisation. With our outer light we want to go towards God. With our inner light we see and feel that we do not have to go towards God because we already are in God and God is already in us; we see and feel that God is our highest and most illumined part. With our outer light we feel God is a Goal to be realised. With our inner light we feel that not only is God our own, but God is the essence and substance of our own reality.

No flattery,
However delightful,
Can charm a true seeker
Of the infinite Light
Even for a fleeting second,
For he has already escaped
The snare of temptation.

The inner experience of light tells us that human life is a constant unfulfilling want whereas the divine life is a constant fulfilling and fulfilled achievement.

There are many ways to transform human nature. One way is to bring down into the system the divine, all-illumining Light of the Supreme, enlarging one's receptivity-vessel. Before human nature is transformed, it is full of darkness. Darkness can be removed only by bringing in light, and not by anything else. We have to bring down light from above consciously and constantly and then expand our receptivity. The more we expand our receptivity, the more we can hold light inside ourselves.

A soul of silence-light
Is indeed
Sovereign on earth.

Once we have had the inner experience of light, we actually do live in Heaven on earth: we live in the heart of eternal Time and in the lap of Immortality.

Another way to transform human nature is to see the divine light in each human being and not to see anything else. Just because we see something undivine in ourselves and in others it has become impossible for us to transform either our own nature or human nature in general. But no matter what they do, what they say or what they are, if we consciously and constantly see only the divine light in others— the light we are bringing down from above—then automatically human nature has to be transformed. If we see light in each individual and in our own nature, then it is not only possible but also inevitable to transform human nature and earth's nature. While bringing down light and enlarging our receptivity and while seeing light inside others, we transform human nature and our own nature.

Before the end of day
My eye of light shall change
My face of somber clay
And touch my spirit's range.

August

Devotion

AUGUST 1

There is no other way to make conscious and constant progress in the spiritual life except to offer your intense devotion constantly to the Pilot Supreme within you.

Devotion is the complete submission of the individual will to the Will divine. Devotion is adoration. Adoration is the spontaneous delight that springs from the heart. Who can be the object of our adoration? God. How can we adore Him? Through our self-surrender.

My dear Lord,
I wish to be led
Every day.
My sweet Lord,
I wish to be led
In every way.
My beloved Lord,
I wish to be led
All the way.

Devotion is blessedness itself. This blessedness is the self-dedicating love turned towards God, seeking to serve Him constantly and unconditionally so that He can be fulfilled both in Heaven and on earth.

Devotion is a soul-stirring emotion. It dynamically permeates the entire consciousness of the devotee. Devotion is action. This action is always inspired by the devotee's inner being.

Devotion brings in renunciation. True renunciation is never a life of isolation. Renunciation is an utter distaste for the animal life of the flesh. It is also a total absence of the ego. A life of true renunciation is a life that lives in the world but does not derive its values from the world.

Are you tired of being who you are?
Are you?
Then give God, for the first time,
A chance to take care of you.
God can easily take care of you,
And He will definitely do it.
Just give Him a chance.

AUGUST 3

I repeat God's Name, not because I feel that by repeating God's Name I shall be able to unseal God's Ears, but because I see Him in different forms of inner beauty each time I repeat His Name.

The manifestations of devotion are simplicity, sincerity, spontaneity, beauty and purity. The manifestations of devotion are one's intense, devoted feeling for one's object of adoration and one's consecrated oneness with the Inner Pilot.

I shall listen to Your Command, I shall.
In Your sky I shall fly, I shall fly.
Eternally You are mine, my very own.
You are my heart's wealth.
For You at night in tears I shall cry,
For You at dawn with light I shall smile.
For You, for You, Beloved, only for You.

Five all-completing words: "Lord, I love You only."

I walk along the road of love, devotion and surrender. First, I offer my love to God, then I offer my devotion to God and finally I offer my surrender to God. When I offer my love to God, I feel that He is the only one whose love I need in order to make progress. When I love Him, I discover that He is none other than my own self, my higher existence, my most illumined existence. Normally, when we love someone, it is a different individuality and personality that we love. But when we love God, we feel that He is our own highest, most illumined Reality.

> *You have anchored your heart*
> *In the infinite Love of God.*
> *Therefore*
> *You do not have to worry*
> *About anything*
> *In the world of dreams*
> *Or in the world of realities.*

Devotion is dedication. Dedication gives a devotee his self-fulfilment. Self-fulfilment is God's Infinitude.

Please do not be forgetful of your great promise to God. Before you came into the world, before you donned the human cloak, you told God, your sweet Lord, with all the sincerity at your command, that you would participate in His divine Play. He said to you, "My child, fulfil Me and fulfil yourself at the same time on earth." You were divinely thrilled; your joy knew no bounds. You said, "Father, I shall. May my soulful promise be worthy of Your compassionate Command."

My Lord,
You have made me happy
By making me Your servant.
Will you not make me
Infinitely happier
By making me Your slave?

AUGUST 6

I love God for God's sake. Him to please in His own Way, I exist on earth.

In the spiritual life, the name of the sunlit path is devotion. This path is definitely the shortcut to God-realisation. It is true that God and His mysteries are beyond the comprehension of speech and intellect. But it is equally true that God is easily accessible through devotion.

My heart will not fade away
Because I have
Carefully placed its beauty
Inside my Lord's Compassion-Heart,
And cheerfully placed its fragrance
At my Lord's Salvation-Feet.

To live a devoted life is to be a conscious child of God's Will.

A true devotee gets great joy when he feels, "All this am I." He gets greater joy when he feels, "All this art Thou." He gets the greatest joy when he feels, "Thou art the Master, I am only the instrument." He who follows the path of knowledge says to God, "Father I want You." He who follows the path of devotion says to God, "Father, I need You." The former says to God, "Father, I own You." The latter says to God, "Father, You own me."

My Lord Supreme,
Do give me the capacity
To look at You at every moment
And not just whenever I would like
To look at You.

Every day breathe a soulful prayer to God. Then you can become sleeplessly faithful to God's Vision-Light.

As in other paths, in the sunlit path the devotee learns that it does not matter how long he prays and meditates, but how he prays and meditates. If he prays and meditates upon the Divine sincerely and unreservedly, then he prays and meditates ten times at once.

When I pray,
I kneel down
Devotedly and secretly.

When I meditate,
I lift up my heart
Soulfully and perfectly.

AUGUST 9

My only responsibility is to fulfil the Will of God.

Like everyone else, a devoted aspirant has needs. But his needs and God's Love and Compassion are always seen together. A real devotee has come to realise that he loves God not to fulfil his human desires but to fulfil God in God's own Way. For an unaspiring person, life is punishment, pure torture. For an aspiring soul, each moment in life is an opportunity for self-illumination and God-fulfilment. In the sunlit path of devotion, the aspirant knows that just as he is hungry for God's infinite Compassion, even so is God hungry for his constant feeling of conscious oneness with Him.

I said what I meant:
"My Lord is all Compassion."
I meant what I said:
"I shall definitely grow into
A perfect instrument of God."

If you always ask God's Benediction, then He will teach you how to do your inner homework.

A child does not care to know what his mother is. He just wants his mother's constant presence of love before him. Similar is the devotee's feeling for his Lord. Many come forward to help him in his life's journey. But he cares not for their help. God's Grace is his sole help and refuge. The tortures of hell are too weak to torment him while he is there with his Lord. His life in hell is a life of perfect bliss. His sufferings and tribulations in Heaven know no bounds if he is there without his Lord beside him.

I yearn and ache for Thee.
Every day I become
Love-seed,
Devotion-plant,
Surrender-tree.

O Lord, forget me not
In my outer goalless wandering
Far and wide.
O Lord, make my pilgrim-heart
The voyager of self-discovery,
The emperor of life-mastery.

Devotion intensifies the seeker's inner hunger, purifies his outer greed and solidifies his integral perfection.

Unlike others, a devotee sincerely feels that he has nothing else in his possession save his desire for God. His desire is his jewel. God's Grace is His jewel. In offering his jewel to God, the devotee binds God. In giving His jewel to His devotee, God liberates and fulfils him.

> *God and I have played*
> *Our respective roles.*
> *I have deepened my faith*
> *In Him.*
> *He has completely comforted*
> *My heart.*

My age-old fear's torture is now being transformed into my heart's rapture. How? Just by virtue of my purest acceptance of God.

We want only to be what God is, that is to say infinite Peace, infinite Light and infinite Bliss. We do not want anything from the world. If the world tortures us, disappoints us or misunderstands us, that is up to the world. We do not expect anything from the world, but we do expect one thing from ourselves, and that one thing is that we will grow into God Himself.

I sing because You sing.
I smile because You smile.
Because You play on the flute
I have become Your flute.
You play in the depths of my heart.
You are mine, I am Yours.
This is my sole identification.
In one form
You are my Mother and Father eternal,
And Consciousness-moon,
Consciousness-sun all-pervading.

Do you know what actually happens when you pray soulfully? When you pray soulfully, you start resembling your Beloved Supreme more and more.

Every time we think of God, we should feel that He is our Ideal, He is our Goal. At the same time, we have to know that to see the Goal is not the aim, to reach the Goal is not the aim. Our aim is to become the Goal itself. God expects nothing short of this from us. He wants us to be what He is. If this is our aim, then when we think of God, when we pray to God, when we meditate on God, God feels that our thought, our prayer and our meditation are absolutely right, absolutely divine.

I pray to God to give me
His Moon's silver Feet.
I meditate on God to give me
His Sun's golden Eye.

From now on, I shall always remain devoted to my life within.

Think of the Supreme. You will feel that your life is of some meaning. Meditate on the Supreme. You will feel that God needs you. Offer yourself to the Supreme. You will feel that the Supreme has already offered His Life-Breath and very Existence to you, to the seeker in you, for all Eternity.

Do you want to hear
What you say during your sleep?
You say that you love God alone
And need God alone, nobody else.

When you say the name of God, immediately God's divine qualities—purity, peace, love, bliss and many others—enter into you.

God is my personal experience. In Him is my life's confidence. With me is His assurance in life and death, and beyond time and space. I live for God. I live to serve Him with my heart's surrender and with my soul's joy. He lives for me. He lives to present me with His all-transcending Vision, to transform my existence into His Heavenly Reality.

Sweet is my Lord
Because He is knowable.
Sweeter is my Lord
Because He is known.
Sweetest is my Lord
Because He invites me
To play hide-and-seek with Him
Every day.

A devotee sees a circle which is God. He enters into it with his soul's cry. He then silently comes and stands at the centre of the circle and grows into a tree of ecstasy.

Oneness, oneness, oneness! O my Beloved Supreme, I have only one need: oneness. I shall be happy if my oneness-need is fulfilled. I shall be equally happy if my oneness-need is not fulfilled. I shall be happy even if it is not fulfilled because the very quest, the very longing for oneness with You, my Source, gives me abundant joy, boundless joy, infinite joy. Let me have this quenchless thirst, this thirst for conscious and constant oneness with You.

O my heart,
Run into God's Vastness infinite.
O my soul,
Soar beyond, far beyond,
The skies of knowledge-light.

Self-love mars the fertile soil of aspiration and renders it sterile. But devotion towards God kindles the mounting flame of aspiration, creating a new world for the aspirant in God, and a new world for God in the aspirant.

O my Beloved Supreme, even if You do not fulfil my oneness-quest, no harm. Just allow the flame of longing for oneness with You to burn in me forever and forever. In the inner world, all I have is You. In the outer world, all I need is You. May my inner world and my outer world become one. In their oneness I shall achieve satisfaction, which is perfection itself. Oneness, oneness, oneness!

I think of God
Because I need Him unavoidably.

God thinks of me
Because He loves me sleeplessly
Plus unconditionally.

Long for anything divine, and it will immediately start to approach you.

Where is God? Who is God? How to realise God? All these questions can easily be answered when we listen to the dictates of the soul. With prayer and meditation we can dive deep within and hear the constant message of and from the soul—the perennial message of light, truth and bliss. Through our prayer and meditation we can embody peace, light and bliss in infinite measure and then, like the soul, we can also enjoy Immortality here on earth as we enjoy it already in Heaven.

My Lord,
My entire being
Is dying to clasp Your Feet
As its only satisfaction.

Man loves. He expects love in return. A devotee loves. But he loves human beings for the sake of his sweet Lord who abides in all. His love breathes in humility, spontaneous joy and selfless service.

When I live inside my heart-universe, I feel the Presence of my Beloved Supreme constantly. Out of His boundless Bounty He appears before me and I see His Face. Him I see with my human eyes; Him I feel with my human heart. I ask my Lord Supreme to grant me His constant Blessings. He says that He has already granted me His Blessings infinite. He tells me to give Him what I have and what I am devotedly, soulfully, unreservedly and unconditionally. I give Him what I have and what I am: ignorance. He, out of His infinite Compassion, gives me what He has and what He is: Delight in infinite measure.

If we think of God sleeplessly,
Then let us love Him unconditionally.
If we love God unconditionally,
Then let us think of Him sleeplessly.

Try to be a person who every day asks himself why he is on earth: to be a slave of man, to be a slave of oneself or to be a chosen child of God. Make the correct choice, and then remain absolutely faithful to that choice.

"By devotedly seeing Me once a day if you get joy, then for that joy I shall give you seventy out of a hundred. By constantly thinking of Me if you get joy, then for that joy I shall give you eighty out of a hundred. By soulfully working for Me if you get joy, then for that joy I shall give you ninety out of a hundred. But by devotedly, constantly, soulfully and inseparably feeling that you are of Me and of Me alone, you get one hundred out of a hundred."

Six things I do every morning:
I energise my body,
I direct my vital,
I inspire my mind,
I open my heart,
I obey my soul,
I renew my unconditional surrender
To my Beloved Supreme.

Divine devotion is our inner urge to do something with utmost sincerity, purity and divinity.

My Beloved Lord Supreme, my Beloved Lord Supreme, will I ever be able to become a perfect instrument of Yours?

"My child, you will without fail become not only a perfect instrument of Mine but a supremely perfect instrument of Mine at My choice Hour. How can My own Divinity's transcendental Vision in you, with you and for you fail? No, My Vision is bound to succeed, My child.

"But you can do one thing every day devotedly and soulfully. You can repeat hundreds of times daily, 'My Lord, You are my mind-sincerity's All, You are my heart-purity's All, You are my life-duty's All.' This will expedite our joint victory."

I shall obey You.
That means You have given me
The capacity to obey You.
I have the capacity to obey You.
That means You are always
Within me and for me.

God, I shall love You unconditionally. God I shall please You eternally in Your own supreme Way.

The aspirant is supposed to meditate early in the morning and he does meditate. What is his meditation? His meditation is his invocation of infinite Light, Peace and Bliss. It is his conscious effort to have nothing to do with the obscurity, impurity, imperfection and ignorance which he sees all around him. He is beyond it; he is above it. During meditation he makes a promise to himself that he will be pure, that he will be detached, that he will constantly aspire. It is his ardent promise to himself that he will not doubt himself, he will not fear anything, he will not be a victim to impurity and anxiety. Every day he makes an inner promise to his soul, to God, that he will be divine, he will be a chosen instrument of God, that he will listen only to the dictates of his inner being.

You may break all the promises
That you have made to humanity,
But never break even one promise to God
If you want to unveil God's Smile on earth
And reveal humanity's cry
In Heaven.

My prayer lies in loving God for His own sake. My prayer is the destroyer of errors, born and unborn.

In order to realise the Goal, in order to reach the Goal deep within, we have to renew our life and make it fresh every day. Each day early in the morning we have to revitalise our outer life with golden hope. This hope is not an idle dream; it is the precursor of the divinity which will manifest in and through our outer nature. It is our dynamic divine quality, our golden hope, that sees the Beyond even when it is still a far cry.

I want to prove to the world
That although my past was only mortal
My present and future
Will be absolutely immortal.

A heart of devotion is purer than the purest flame.

God-realisation means conscious, constant and inseparable oneness with God. You have to know that it is conscious. When you pray and meditate, that is your conscious approach to God. You may not attain oneness, but you are consciously trying to receive Him at that time. Usually when you think of someone, oneness is not there, but when oneness is there, you get tremendous delight. God-realisation has to be conscious, constant and inseparable oneness with the Highest.

Lord,
Even if you stop loving me,
I shall keep on loving You,
For You are my Eternity's Only Beloved Supreme.
Lord,
Even if You stop caring for me,
I shall keep on serving You,
For You are my Eternity's
Only Sovereign Absolute.

Devotion is the beauty of a God-server.

Our inner perfection-life is our constant remembrance of God as the highest Absolute and our feeling of God as the Absolute Transcendental. Our outer perfection-life is our feeling of God as the immanent, omnipresent Universal. When you think of inner perfection, go as high as possible; and when you think of outer perfection, spread your wings and become one with everything else. When you think of inner perfection, think of God within you as the Transcendental Absolute. When you think of earth-perfection, think of God as the Universal Consciousness. When you have established your oneness with the Universal Consciousness, that is the perfection of your outer life; and when you have established your oneness with the Transcendental Height, that is the perfection of your inner life.

Today you have realised
That you, too, need God.
Tomorrow you will realise
That God, too, needs you
To become another God.

You can easily ease God's pain by increasing a little more your heart's cry.

Just before you start meditating, say four things: "Fear, get out of my life! Doubt, get out of my life! Jealousy, get out of my life! Insecurity, get out of my life! I do not need you and I will never need you."

Then they will all come out of you and ask, "Whom do you want?"

"I want only meditation; I want only God," you will say.

> *I think of God first*
> *Before I think of myself.*
> *Why?*
> *Because only God can be*
> *My inspiration-thought.*

> *I love God first*
> *Before I love myself.*
> *Why?*
> *Because only God can be*
> *My satisfaction-love.*

Devotion is our inner sweetness. Devotion is our divine intensity. Devotion is our supreme dynamism.

We must meditate soulfully so that we can increase our faith in our Beloved Supreme. We must meditate soulfully so that our Beloved Supreme can have more confidence in us. Meditation is the most effective way to increase the seeker's faith in his Beloved Supreme and also to increase the confidence of his Beloved Supreme in the seeker.

Sweet is my Lord.
Him I have realised as the Eternal Truth.
Sweeter is my Lord.
Him I have realised as the only Doer.
Sweetest is my Lord.
Him I have realised as the Enjoyer Supreme.

Each devoted moment prepares a beautiful sunrise and a fruitful sunset.

When I pray to the Supreme, I pray with my sincerity-mind. When I meditate on the Supreme, I meditate with my purity-heart. When I love the Supreme, I love with my intensity's life-breath. Three things we do: we pray, we meditate, we love. When we pray, meditate and love, everything is done.

> *Pray soulfully,*
> *Pray sleeplessly.*
> *God is bound to hear*
> *Even your faint*
> *And faltering prayer.*

A heart of devotion is wiser than the wisest sage.

The mind is so tricky. With this tricky mind, we cannot do anything sincerely. But if we can sincerely pray, then we will get everything. The heart is covered by weakness, garbage, rubbish. That is why the heart does not remain pure. But if we can meditate with a pure heart, we will get everything. And if we can love the Supreme with our intensity's life-breath, then the Supreme is caught forever.

As God's Face
And His Grace
Are inseparable,
Even so I want my heart
And my heart's cry
To be inseparable.

Purity's soulful permanence lives in devotion.

Devotion is our soul's fearless quality. Devotion does not mean begging from someone. Devotion means dedicated service to the divine child in us. It means intensity, the intensity that makes us feel one and not the intensity that separates and frustrates us. Devotion means entering into the superior part of one's own existence. Devotion is the sweetest feeling in us, the feeling of oneness with something higher and deeper in us. It is the most intimate connection with our better self, purer self, higher, nobler and deeper self. It is the sweetest awareness of Truth.

At the high tide of his earthly triumph,
He went to Heaven
With his heart's most soulful cry
To sit at God's Compassion-Feet.

Devotion is the secret of secrets. It lets you establish the sweetest and the most intimate connection with God, who entirely belongs to you.

In the spiritual life, if one wants to make quick progress, then I wish to say that devotion is the only answer. If there is devotion in the entire being, then one can drink nectar every day in one's spiritual awakening, spiritual discipline and spiritual realisation. It is devotion that gives us sweetness in our life, and carries us to the Source of life-immortalising nectar.

When you love
With devotion,
You are divinely great.
When you surrender
With devotion,
You are divinely good.
When you pray
With devotion,
You are supremely great.
When you meditate
With devotion,
You are supremely good.
Devotion, devotion, devotion.

September

Gratitude

Gratitude is something in our heart that helps us transcend our experience of earth and intensify our realisation of God.

We are grateful to God, for He is with us here and now. We are grateful to God, for He has created within us a genuine hunger for Him. We are grateful to God, for He has given us a long express train of hope. We are grateful to God, for He has repeatedly told us that He will keep His promise. What is His promise? His promise is that He will not be satisfied unless and until each Creation of His satisfies Him in His own Way.

All my complaints
Turned into gratitude-tears
When my Lord Supreme approached me
With His Smile-flooded Face.

If you want to live in a gratitude-world, then you must free yourself from the temptation-world.

A true seeker offers to God what he has and what he is. What he has is ignorance. What he is, is a gratitude-heart. When he offers his gratitude-heart, he becomes a chosen instrument of the Supreme. A chosen instrument at times pleases God in his own way; at other times he pleases God in God's own Way. There comes a time when the chosen instrument is transformed into an unconditionally surrendered instrument. An unconditionally surrendered instrument of God pleases God at every moment in God's own Way.

He becomes his meditation-heart.
This is his special way
Of thanking God.

One can bring forth gratitude through the constant inner cry.

We cry outwardly when we desperately need name, fame, outer capacity, prosperity and so forth. But when we cry inwardly, we have to feel that we are crying only to please and fulfil God in His own Way. The outer cry is for our own fulfilment, in our own way. The inner cry is for God-fulfilment in God's own Way. If there is a constant inner cry, that means we are trying to please God, satisfy God and fulfil God in God's own Way. If we can cry inwardly, in silence, then our gratitude increases, because inside the inner cry is the abode of gratitude, and inside the abode of gratitude is God.

> *God's favourite meal*
> *Consists of my heart's*
> *Gratitude-tears*
> *And my life's*
> *Satisfaction-smile.*

Stamp your heart with a gratitude-smile. You will really be perfect!

I am grateful to the world because it has given me the opportunity to serve the Supreme. I am grateful to the world because it has given me the opportunity to invoke my Supreme and offer Him to the world at large. I am grateful to the world because it has given me the opportunity to make it feel that God is the only Life, the only Reality, which is humanity's eternal choice and which will eventually become humanity's divinised, perfected and immortalised voice of the Supreme. I am grateful to the world, not because the world has given me what it has—aspiration—but because the world has accepted me as I am. Nothing more, nothing less than what I am, the world expects from me.

O my inexperienced heart,
Try to become the smile
Of gratitude and surrender.
Your unlimited anxiety-worry-world
Will disappear before long.

SEPTEMBER 5

My successful life begins when I feel that I can give God what I am: my gratitude-heart.

Lord Supreme, out of Your infinite Bounty You have chose me to be Your instrument. You could have chosen somebody else to play the role, but You have granted me the golden opportunity. To You I offer my constant gratitude, my gratitude-heart, for You have chosen me to become Your instrument to manifest You here on earth in Your own Way.

A gratitude-heart
Is only a very short distance away
From God-Victory.

This morning I have discovered something absolutely new—my sleeplessly sincere gratitude-heart can alone do the work of my love, devotion and surrender most satis-factorily. My Lord, do give me the capacity to execute my new discovery every day in my life.

Every morning you have to offer your gratitude to God for having awakened your consciousness while others are still sleeping, and for all His infinite Blessings to you. If you offer just a fragment of your gratitude, you will feel God's Compassion. Then, when you feel God's Compassion, try to offer yourself. Say, "I will try to please You only in Your own Way. So far, I have asked you to please me in my own way, to give me this and that so that I can be happy. But today I am asking for the capacity to please You in Your own Way." If you can say this sincerely, automatically your morning meditation will be strengthened.

A gratitude-heart
Every day pioneers a new road
To arrive at compassion-height-palace.

I am happy because I have a heart of love. I am happy because I have a mind of trust. I am happy because I have a life of gratitude.

The Inner Pilot will give you the inspiration and aspiration to become spiritual and He will be able to give you more receptivity if He sees that every day you are increasing your gratitude-capacity. The more you can offer your gratitude to the Supreme Pilot within you, the more and the sooner you will increase your receptivity. Gratitude means self-offering to one's highest self. This gratitude is not going to somebody else; it is going to your own highest self. Gratitude helps us identify and feel our oneness with our own highest reality.

O my gratitude-heart,
You are my indispensable partner.
Together we shall reach
The Satisfaction-Home
Of our Beloved Supreme.

Gratitude is the multiplication of our heart's oneness-love.

The second you offer gratitude in your thoughts and in your feelings, your oneness will be perfect. If you offer gratitude, you will understand more; your mental vision, psychic vision, everything will become perfect. Gratitude, gratitude, gratitude is the only answer. Try to grow the gratitude-flower inside your heart and watch it blossom petal by petal. As it blossoms it is spreading its beauty and fragrance.

If you sow gratitude-seeds
Inside your heart,
Then definitely you will see
Dedication-flames
That will grow up and up
And eventually grow into
A perfection-sun.

You can know God's Will in your daily life if early in the morning you offer your utmost gratitude to God for what He has already done for you.

When you offer your gratitude-heart, then it expands; and when it expands it becomes one with God's Universal Reality. Early in the morning, before you meditate or do anything, offer as much gratitude as possible; offer your soulful tears just because you have become what you are now. If you do this, eventually you will become infinitely more than what you are now. So gratitude will be able to make you feel what God's Will is. God's Will will act in and through you and God will do everything in and through you, and for you, if you offer gratitude.

Your gratitude-heart
Is your soul's most valuable treasure,
And this treasure can never be stolen
By anybody.

The best way to increase our gratitude is to cry more soulfully and more spontaneously than a little child who is crying for milk or for a toy.

Let us take God as a shopkeeper. He sells many things: love, joy, beauty, purity, grace and many, many other things. But in His shop there is one thing that is most expensive, and that is gratitude. When we go to God the shopkeeper, everything we can buy because it is quite cheap. But when we try to buy gratitude, we are shocked when we hear the price. We do not have that much money. Why? Because to buy gratitude, we have to become aspiration itself, dedication itself, devotion itself, surrender itself. Our life of aspiration, dedication, devotion and surrender will be our currency to buy gratitude from God's shop.

The seeker's offering
Of an iota of gratitude to God
Is as beautiful as a rose
Held by God in His own Hand.

God has given me His able Life. I am giving God my active gratitude.

We are under the impression that gratitude is something we have which we are not giving to God; but we are mistaken. We can have nothing to give to God unless and until we have first gotten it from Him. Gratitude has to come from God directly. If God does not give us the sense, the feeling, the flower of gratitude within us, then we can never offer gratitude to Him.

Change your inner attitude.
Collect all the gratitude-flowers
Of your heart.
A new world will open up before you
To help you face tomorrow's night
And change the abysmal fate
Of the day after tomorrow.

Through constant soulful gratitude you can easily invoke your divine qualities.

We must cry to God for the power of gratitude. In the spiritual life, a moment of sincere gratitude to the Supreme is equal to an hour of the most intense aspiration, concentration, meditation and contemplation. Gratitude has the mightiest power to win God, but we have to get it before we can give it.

If you want concern from God,
Then give Him what you have:
Love.
If you want love from God,
Then give Him what you are supposed to be:
A gratitude-heart.

Every morning try to greet God with only one thing: an ever-increasing gratitude-gift.

We all use the word 'gratitude.' We try to make others feel what gratitude means, but we ourselves do not know; we ourselves have never felt it in the strict sense of the term. Everything else has been born in the earth-consciousness, but gratitude has yet to take birth. When divine gratitude takes birth in our human life, God-manifestation will not remain a far cry. When gratitude takes birth in human life, God's Reality will be able to manifest itself on earth.

My Absolute Lord Supreme,
My gratitude-heart is the only place
Where I can see your Compassion-Feet.

Every day we have the golden opportunity to offer our gratitude to our Lord Beloved Supreme in everything we do.

For good things naturally we offer gratitude to God. But even if we have bad experiences, like bad thoughts, still we can show gratitude. There are two ways. One way is to immediately compare what is happening now with a time when we had an even worse experience. We will see that the wrong, undivine, impure thoughts we are having today are nothing in comparison to what we were experiencing on that other horrible day, when we were suffering so terribly. Then we can say, "Right now I am bad, but I am so grateful to God because my consciousness is till much higher than it was on that horrible day." Or we can compare ourselves with the way we were ten years ago. Then we will say, "Oh God, I am so grateful to You that today I am not as bad as I was ten years ago." This is the best way—to compare our own life now with what it used to be.

Exhale the dust
Of the past.
Inhale the fragrance
Of the future.

Slowly and unmistakably you are climbing your heart's gratitude-tree.

Another way to constantly offer gratitude to God is to compare ourselves with the ordinary people who are around us. We can look to this side and that side and immediately see unaspiring people who are infinitely worse than we are. Then we can say, "O God, because of Your Compassion, I am infinitely better than these people. I could have been so bad—like him or her—but You have kept me much better. You are so kind, so compassionate to me."

Now that I have cut down
My heart's ingratitude-tree,
God is opening His Heart-Door
Unconditionally
And will leave it open
Eternally.

Gratitude is one's feeling of concern for the Highest.

As the Highest has concern for the lowest, the lowest also should have some concern for the Highest. We may ask, "What can we do for God with our concern?" We have to know what He will think of us if we live an ordinary, undivine, animal life. The answer is that He will feel miserable. He will think that we are not making any progress and are holding back His Manifestation. Our concern for the Highest makes us feel what we can do, and that very thing is to offer gratitude. This is one way of viewing gratitude.

At night
He dreams only God-dreams,
And during the day
His life becomes
A sleepless wave of gratitude.

The latest arrival at Heaven's gate is my life's gratitude-heart.

There is another way to view gratitude. When we are about to be totally destroyed, our hope, our pride, everything that we have is shattered and smashed. But inside our utter hopelessness, helplessness, destruction and frustration, if we see a streak of hope, a streak of light, that hope or that light is gratitude. Like a magnet, our iota of light is pulling down a higher force which is entering into us to save us. The moment we have this magnet, it pulls down more of God's Grace and God's Love. The magnet is our inner cry, our gratitude, bringing down more Love from above.

If you take
God's Affection and Love
With thankfulness,
Then you will indisputably become
Both great and good.

How to melt God's Heart? Just launder your life with gratitude-soap.

The unfortunate thing is that our human mind feels that gratitude is something inferior. We feel that when we offer gratitude to God, because He offered us something first, we are doing something inferior. If someone has done something for us, naturally we will show him our gratitude, but we feel that the power of gratitude is inferior to the power of giving.

God gave me something special:
Awareness.
I gave God something special:
Willingness.
Now God wants to give me
His Satisfaction
And I want to give God
My gratitude.

My Lord Supreme, I am all gratitude to You because You have given my heart the readiness to accept You.

God sees Himself and us as one. He feels that He is giving what He has—Love and Compassion—and we are giving what we have—gratitude. Our power of gratitude is every bit as strong as His Light and Love-Power. In the beginning of the Game, He gave us what He wanted to give us, which is gratitude, and He kept for Himself His Light. Now, the Role He has is to offer us Light and our role is to offer Him gratitude. When He is giving us His Light and we are giving Him our gratitude, then only can we manifest.

Gratitude carries the message of Immortality
And enters into God's Heart
To see God's universal Satisfaction-Smile.

My Lord Supreme, I am all gratitude to You because You have given my mind the willingness to wait for You.

How do you develop gratitude? Not by looking into the far past. What were you in the past? A bundle of desire, a bundle of jealousy, a bundle of insecurity and a bundle of falsehood. But now what have you become? Are you the same Himalayan falsehood? No, far from it. Now you are in the truth, of the truth and for the truth. What has made you feel that you are in the truth, of the truth and for the truth or for the highest life? The answer will be your inner cry. And who has given you this inner cry? God.

Never become lost
In your unaspiring past.
Do not become tired of knocking
At your heart's new door.

I am extremely grateful to my Beloved Supreme, for He has given me the prayer-capacity to become one with the Christ Consciousness.

Now, what will you give God, since He has given you so much inner cry? You can give the thing that you feel is best. What God feels best to give you is His Compassion. Because of His Compassion you have accepted the spiritual life. What you should feel best to give Him in return is your gratitude. Your gratitude is by far your best quality, so give Him your gratitude. The more you give gratitude to Him, the more you will be able to receive from Him.

> *There are many ways*
> *To see the Face of God.*
> *But there is only one way*
> *To sit at the Feet of God,*
> *And that way is to breathe in constantly*
> *The breath of gratitude.*

I am extremely grateful to my Beloved Supreme, for He has given me the dedication-capacity to become one with the Buddha Consciousness.

To develop perfect gratitude, first of all, please try to feel that gratitude abides inside your heart. Then ask yourself whether you are in the heart. The immediate answer will be, "One minute a day." The rest of the time, you are the mind or you are the body or you are the vital. But if you can feel that you are the heart, not just for a fleeting second or a fleeting minute, but twenty-four hours a day, if you can feel the presence of your heart as your own existence, then easily you will have gratitude, since gratitude lives inside the heart.

Stamp your heart
With a gratitude-smile.
You will really be perfect!

I am extremely grateful to my Beloved Supreme for He has given me the perfection-capacity to become one with the Krishna Consciousness.

How can you increase your gratitude? If you have the capacity to feel that you are the heart, try to feel that your heart is constantly becoming large, larger, largest. It is like the father whose salary is constantly increasing. In the same way, the capacity of your heart is constantly increasing. When the father becomes richer, the child also becomes richer because he knows that his father's property belongs to him as well. So when the heart is all the time expanding, when its capacity is all the time increasing, gratitude is also increasing and growing in capacity.

He who has a gratitude-heart
Will realise
That God's Delight in him
Is God's never-ending
Beginning.

I am extremely grateful to my Beloved Supreme, for He has given me the satisfaction-capacity to become one with Him, with His Consciousness that is already manifested and with His Consciousness that is yet to be manifested.

Once you have a perfection-tree, if you want to keep it in perfect condition, you have to offer gratitude at every moment. You touch the root of the tree and offer gratitude. With gratitude you touch the foot of the tree, the trunk of the tree, the branches of the tree, the flowers of the tree, the fruits of the tree. When your heart's gratitude comes to the fore, when you become all gratitude, this gratitude is like a flow, a flow of consciousness. When your consciousness is flowing, feel that this gratitude-flow is like a river that is watering the root of the tree and the tree itself. So always it is through gratitude that your consciousness-river will flow and water the perfection-tree inside you.

A gratitude-heart
Will unmistakably be invited
To God's Immortality-Feast.

I am grateful to my Beloved Supreme, for out of His infinite Bounty He has given me the capacity to love Him more than I love myself.

The most important thing to maintain the inner cry is to offer your gratitude every second to the Supreme. Your inner cry comes from God's Concern and Compassion. When you offer your gratitude, immediately your cry increases; it becomes continuous and constant. When you offer gratitude, your inner cry mounts to the highest.

There was a time
When I was grateful
To those who took my side,
Although I was quite often wrong.
But now I am grateful
Only to those who take God's side,
No matter how feeble they are,
No matter how idle they are.

I am grateful to my Beloved Supreme, for out of His infinite Bounty, He has given me the capacity not to drag Him into my desire-world, but to implore His Presence in my aspiration-world, and also to offer Him my earth-bound will and desire-life, and soulfully declare, "Let Thy Will be done."

When God fulfils your desire, you are all gratitude. When God does not fulfil your desire, if you can become all gratitude to Him, then God Himself is bound to come to you, not only to replace and fulfil your desire, but to give you what He has and what He is: Infinitude.

To tie me to God
God has
His Compassion-Sun
And I have my
Gratitude-flames.

I am grateful to my Beloved Supreme, for out of His infinite Bounty, He has given me the capacity to feel His Need more than my own need.

We are on earth, here and now, only to please God in God's own Way. It is a difficult task indeed, but we get joy only when we cross hurdles. If we do not do everything here and now, then there will be no beginning of tomorrow's new journey. This new journey and the journey's goal will come and greet us, for the achievements of the soul and the journey's goal are inseparable. When we cry with gratitude, it is the journey's soul that acts in and through us, which is a splendid achievement. And when we smile with gratitude, it is the journey's goal that has become one with aspiration's starting point and with aspiration's ever-transcending horizon.

Your mind does only one thing:
Every day it writes
Gratification-letters to itself.
Your heart does only one thing:
Every day it writes
A gratitude-letter to God.

The petals of my heart-rose I shall turn into my life's gratitude-tears.

When you feel gratitude, feel that a flower, a lotus or a rose, is blooming inside of you, petal by petal, and when you feel tremendous gratitude, then feel that the flower has totally blossomed.

> *The beauty of the rose*
> *Needs no recommendation.*
> *The fragrance of my gratitude-heart*
> *Needs no recommendation either.*

I shall be extremely, extremely grateful to my Beloved Supreme the day I can feel that my soul-bird lives only for Him inside my body-cage here on earth and there in Heaven.

We can offer gratitude to God no matter what kind of consciousness we have. If we are not having good thoughts, we can say, "O God, I am grateful to You because no matter how bad I am now, I was infinitely worse a few years ago. Because of Your Compassion I have become at least a human being."

Your heart's gratitude-flames
Can and will create
An invisible power
Which will one day be visible
Even to your naked human eyes.

I shall be extremely, extremely and extremely grateful to my Beloved Supreme the day I can declare to the world within and to the world without that I am what He has and I have what He is.

When we reach the Transcendental Goal, we see that God and we are one and will forever remain one. Man and God, the aspirant in man and the saviour in God, are totally one. Each fulfils the other. One fulfils through his soul's gratitude; the other fulfils through His Soul's infinite Compassion. Gratitude and Compassion fulfil each other—gratitude from the aspiring soul of man and Compassion from the illumining Soul of God.

Aspiration begins.
Surrender continues.
Gratitude concludes.

October

Surrender

Surrender is the most suitable net to entrap the Divine. It is at once wisdom and power in action.

In surrender we feel the absolute acceptance of the Divine and the Supreme. If we surrender our life totally and say, "God, I place my life entirely at Your Feet," then our whole existence enters into God. God is omniscient, God is omnipotent, God is infinite, so our surrender immediately becomes the Omniscient, the Omnipotent and the Infinite. Surrender is the quickest road to oneness with God. If we can jump into the ocean of peace and bliss, then we will become one with God.

Now that he is
A choice instrument of God,
He devotedly hears
When God tiptoes
Across his heart.

Love is sweet, devotion is sweeter, surrender is sweetest.

In surrender we say, "No matter what God wants to give me, no matter what He wants to do with my life, I am ready. I fully surrender with my very breath, my very existence. Even if God does not want my help, my life or my existence, I will be happy." At that time the disciple wants only the Will of God, the Supreme. This is true surrender.

I shall not use anymore
My common sense,
For my common sense
Is a common thing
Which everybody has.
From now on I shall use
Only one sense:
My surrender-sense,
Which lives only in God
And only for God.

OCTOBER 3

Surrender to God's Will is the highest realisa-tion of our hidden power.

It is very easy to say, "Let Thy Will be done." But when we say this, we have to identify ourselves with God's Will. How? Through surrender. If we really surrender, then we become one with God's Will. In the spiritual life, there can be no better achievement and no more powerful weapon than surrender.

If God's Way
Is the right way,
Then my way, too
Can be the right way.
How?
Just by following sleeplessly
God's Way.

Since God's Way
Is not so difficult,
Then let me surrender
My way to God's Way.
Then my way immediately becomes
As easy as God's Way,
God's perfect Way.

Surrender is God's God-Power in His own tiny human body.

Surrender is an unfoldment. It is the unfoldment of our body, mind and heart into the sun of divine plenitude within us. Surrender to this inner sun is the greatest triumph of life. The hound of failure cannot reach us when we are in that sun. The prince of evil fails to touch us when we have realised and founded our oneness with that eternally life-giving sun. Surrender knows that there is a guiding Hand and feels that this guiding Hand is ever present. This Hand may strike or bless the aspirant, but the surrendered aspirant has discovered the truth that whatever comes from the Supreme is always fruitful of good and light.

How do I occupy my time?
I teach my heart
How to write surrender-letters
With love-pen
To my Beloved Supreme.

My successful day begins when I feel that I can give God what I have: my surrender-life.

Our surrender is a most precious thing. God alone deserves it. We can offer our surrender to another individual, but only for the sake of realising God. If that individual has reached his Goal, he can help us in our spiritual journey. However, if we offer ourselves to someone just to satisfy that person, then we are committing a Himalayan blunder. What we should do is offer ourselves unreservedly to the Lord in him. Every action of ours should be to please God and not to gain applause. Our actions are too secret and sacred to display before others. They are meant for our own progress, achievement and realisation. There is no limit to our surrender.

From today on
I shall try to have
A new type of success.
My conscious surrender
To the Will of my Beloved Supreme
Will be my only success.

When we are conscious of our inner existence, only then can we be guided by God's Compas-sion.

You constantly surrender to earthly things—noise, the traffic lights, the government. You feel that you are totally lost if you do not surrender to these things, whereas if you do surrender, at least you can maintain your existence on earth. Whatever the earth gives you, even if it is a form of torture, you feel that you have to accept it. If you want to lead an aspiring life, then you have to have this same kind of feeling toward spiritual things. You have to feel that if you do not pray, if you do not meditate, then you will be totally lost; if you do not cry, if you do not surrender to the higher divinity, then your whole existence will be of no value. You have to feel that without the inner guidance you are totally helpless and lost. And this inner guidance comes only when you really want to surrender your ignorance to the Light within you.

There can be
No better start in life
Than to surrender your expectations
To God's Will.

Divine surrender is the surrender we make to our own highest part.

Aspiring people will try to go beyond earthly circumstances and events and surrender to their inner divinity. This is not the surrender of a slave to the master; it is not a helpless surrender. Here one surrenders his imperfections, limitations, bondage and ignorance to his highest Self, which is flooded with peace, light and bliss.

> *I shall surrender my I-ness at Your Feet.*
> *I shall accept Your I-ness in my dream.*
> *I shall see the waves of peace in Your Eyes.*
> *I shall bind You with my sweet awakening.*
> *O Beauty Supreme, in my life and death*
> *I shall only fly Your Victory-Banner.*

OCTOBER 8

It is through identification of one's will with the divine Will that receptivity automatically increases.

In real surrender we feel that our darkest part is surrendering to our brightest part, that our unlit part is surrendering to our fully illumined part. Let us say that my feet are in darkness and my head is in light. My feet are surrendering to my head, knowing perfectly well that both the feet and the head are parts of the same body. This is the surrender of oneness. One enters into surrender knowing well that the brighter part is equally his.

Surrender suffers no loss.
Surrender suffers no failure.
Surrender suffers no unworthiness.

OCTOBER 9

The more complete the aspirant's surrender, the brighter the smile of his psychic being.

To have true dependence, one has to feel that he is hopeless without the divine Grace of the Supreme. If your dependence is absolutely sincere, if you feel that without the help of the Supreme you cannot breathe, then this is surrender. When you breathe in, you depend on your life-breath. If your life-breath goes away, then you do not exist. Similarly, if you can feel that you are totally depending on the Will of the Supreme, which is far more important than your life-breath, then this dependence is true surrender.

An unconditional surrender-head
Wears the crown
Of God-Delight.

God has given me the surrender needed to obey Him in the night of the finite and in the Light of the Infinite.

There comes a time in our spiritual life when we realise that we are not satisfied with what we have, whether it is material wealth or inner wealth, or with what we are. At that time we are ready for surrender. How does one surrender? It is very easy. When we feel the need for surrender, automatically the means will come. If we are desperately in need of surrender, if we feel the soul's inner urge, if our entire being wants to surrender to God's Will, then automatically we will be given more than the necessary capacity, assurance, compassion and light from above and within. When we surrender, we empty all our impurity into God and He replaces it with His Purity and His Divinity.

He who is pleasing God
In God's own Way
Will find all earthly and Heavenly
Experiences in his life agreeable.

In life there are many questions, but surrender to God's Will is the only answer.

Surrender to God's Will entirely depends on our necessity. If we feel that our life is meaningless, that we will not be satisfied or fulfilled without surrendering our earthly existence to God's Will, then surrender will be possible for us. God can never compel us to surrender; it is we who have to feel the necessity of loving God and devoting ourselves to God at every second.

Those who want to please the Supreme
In His own Way
Will have Heaven's fastest
Satisfaction-speed.
Those who do not want
To please the Supreme in His own Way
Will have earth's slower than the slowest
Frustration-destruction-speed.

When my heart unreservedly and soulfully obeys God's Will and I accept it as my own will, infinite joy grows within my heart and eternal joy flows through my heart.

If there is total surrender, then there can be no failure. Surrender means the greatest joy, deepest joy, most soulful joy, even in so-called failure. Success also brings the same joy. When we are successful in something, immediately we derive joy from our success. Similarly, if our inner and outer lives are surcharged with surrendering light, then at every moment we derive pure unalloyed joy from the highest Source. If we have this kind of spontaneous inner joy, then we can feel that it comes only from our total surrender to the Inner Pilot, the Master, the Guru, God.

Why do you not just surrender?
You will see
That a life of surrender
Is the only way
To make you
Perfectly plus permanently happy.

In life, everything may fail us, but not sur-render. Surrender has a free access to God's Omnipotence. Hence the path of surrender is the perfect perfection of protection.

Divine surrender, from the spiritual point of view, comes from will-power. If we have an adamantine will, then we will get the capacity to make unconditional surrender. Again, if we can surrender unconditionally to God, then we will get the capacity to develop will-power. Inner will power, which is the soul's light, and surrender, which is the oneness of our heart with the Absolute, always go together. They are inseparable. There can be no difference between the soul's will-power and the unconditional surrender of our entire being to the Will of the Supreme. Both are equally strong.

This world has nothing for you.
Suddenly, one day you will start going
Your own way.
Your way, too, will have nothing
For you.
Eventually, you will start going God's Way,
For that is the only way.

From now on, my life of surrender to God's Will will be my infallible guide.

To have peace in abundant measure, we have to surrender our earth-bound will to the Heaven-free Will of God. We have to cheerfully, soulfully, devotedly, unreservedly and unconditionally surrender our limited human reality to the Universal or Transcendental Reality. This surrender is not like the surrender of a slave to his master. This surrender is based on the wisdom-light that recognizes a difference between our own highest height and our own lowest depth. Both the highest and the lowest belong to us. When we surrender our will to the Will of the Supreme, we offer our lowest part to our highest part, for the Supreme is none other than our own highest Self.

In the spiritual life
A surrender-life
Is the only source of a satisfaction-heart.

If we can make unconditional surrender to God's Will, we immediately know what God wants from us and what He wants us to do.

Let us try to satisfy the Supreme in us in His own Way cheerfully, soulfully and unconditionally. If we please Him in our own way even one time out of one hundred, we shall feel miserable because that one time we will be separated from our Source. For a sincere seeker, to remain separated from his Source even for a fleeting second is to suffer excruciating pangs. Therefore, let us try to satisfy the Supreme at every moment in His own Way.

If you are
Completely awakened,
Then for you
There is but one way:
God's Way,
Only God's Way.

When God's Will is my will, I have not to give up anything, for He is with everything and in everything.

How can we conquer forms of temptation? We can conquer them only by surrendering—not to them, but to the divine Light, to the divine Will. How can we do this? We can do it by consciously trying during our meditation to feel that we are the instrument and somebody else is the player. And who is that somebody? It is the Inner Pilot. If we feel that we are the doer, the undivine forces will mock us. They will come and make us proud, haughty, undivine, impure and insecure. So we have to pray to the Supreme during our meditation: "O Lord, I am Your instrument. I am so grateful that You have made me a conscious instrument. Please use me in Your own Way."

My outer life
Shall never succeed
And my inner life
Shall never proceed
Unless I invent
A totally new surrender-way.

If surrender is our approach to God-realisation, then we will realise God most easily and most quickly.

There are two types of surrender. One type of surrender comes under compulsion. This is the surrender of a slave to his master. He knows that if he does not serve his master, if he is not constantly at his master's beck and call, he will be punished. This surrender is based on fear. But the divine surrender is otherwise. Here we surrender our ignorance, incapacity and imperfection to the Inner Pilot, who is all Light, all Illumination, all Perfection. When we enter into the spiritual life, we come to realise that when we surrender to our ignorance, we are just surrendering our lowest reality to our own highest Reality. This surrender is based on love and oneness.

What has saved and illumined my life?
Not my possession-life,
But my cheerful surrender-breath
To my Lord's Will.

Prayer is best expressed in my day-to-day life when my prayer has become a spontaneous, self-giving surrender to the Will of God.

When we pray and meditate, we discover a kind of divine surrender within us which makes us feel that God and we are essentially one. He is our Eternal Father; He is our most illumined part, our Source, which we are now climbing up to and entering into. So, by surrendering, we do not lose anything; on the contrary, we return to our Source and become what we originally were. The finite consciously and cheerfully enters into the Infinite. Each one of us is now like a tiny drop. When it enters into the ocean, a tiny drop loses its individuality and becomes one with the infinite expanse of the ocean.

Surrender to your higher life.
Your lower life will be blessed
With a beautiful Smile from God
And your higher life will be blessed
With a new Message from God.

Absolute surrender to the Divine is the only strength that can help an aspirant to wrestle with all the outer and inner problems of life.

We do not surrender our identity; we surrender only our limited, earth-bound individuality, the individuality that binds us, that says "I and mine," instead of "we." What we do is develop our conscious identity with God and God's Will, in order to achieve an inseparable oneness with Him. At that time we do not worry about losing our puny human individuality, for we gain God's infinite vastness in its place.

Everything has to be done
On the basis of surrender.
Whatever we may do
Without surrender
Will remain utterly meaningless.

The supreme prayer says, "Lord, give me, if so is Your Will; take me, if so is Your Will. I have only one message for You: I am all for You, only for You."

On the strength of his sincere aspiration, a true seeker says, "O God, if You feel that I should have Your Vision, if You feel that You want to fulfil Yourself in me and through me, if You feel that You can utilise me as Your instrument, I am at Your service. If You want me to stand before You, I shall come and stand. If You want to stand before me, I shall be equally happy. If You do not want either, but want somebody else to stand before You, I shall still be happy." This is what we call surrender. This is the ultimate surrender.

Like your heart,
You can be happy
Only when you ask God
How things can be done
In God's own Way.

When the divine call comes, you have to give up everything. Then, when you give up every-thing, you get the Infinite.

An aspirant has to know his goal. If his goal is God-realisation, he can start with that in mind. But the ultimate Goal is unconditional surrender to God's Will. When God sees that His child, His most devoted child, has made this unconditional surrender—not for a second, not for a day or year, but for a whole life-time, for all incarnations to come, for all Eternity— then alone God embraces His dearest, His sweetest, His most devoted child. And when that embrace takes place, man changes into God Himself.

Surrender your common sense:
That you are only a human being.
Surrender your earthly goal:
Name and fame.
Receive immediately what God has for you:
His Eternity's Immortality-Crown.

A perfect renunciation and a complete self-surrender are the obverse and reverse of an ambrosial coin.

How can we know something is God's Will? When something is God's Will, we will feel a kind of inner joy or satisfaction before we start doing it. While working, we will also get joy. Finally, we feel that we will be equally happy if our action is fruitful or fruitless. In the ordinary life we are happy only when success dawns. Only when we see victory at the end of our journey are we happy and delighted. But if we can have the same kind of happiness, joy and satisfaction whether we succeed or fail, and if we can cheerfully offer the result of our actions at the Feet of our Beloved Supreme, then only can we know that what we have done is God's Will. Otherwise, when there is success, we feel that what we did was God's Will, and when there is failure, we say that what we did was the will of a hostile force. Or when we succeed we say it is because of our personal effort, our will, and when we fail we say it is because God does not care for the result.

You are bound to know God's Will
If you allow God
To become real to you.

If you have surrendered to God all that you have and all that you are, then only can you feel that God is responsible for all your activities.

We can blame God at our sweet will. We can mis-understand Him at our sweet will. When we fail, we can blame God, and when we succeed, we can try to get the glory for ourselves. But if we are sincere seekers and if we want real, abiding happiness, then we shall do the things that we feel are good and right, and the results we shall offer to the Supreme. Success and failure are two experiences. These two experiences we have to unify, and whichever experience we get at the end of our endeavour, we have to offer to the Supreme with tremendous joy. If we can place the result at the Feet of our Beloved Supreme soul-fully, cheerfully, unreservedly and unconditionally, then without fail we will have true peace of mind. At that time peace of mind will come and knock at our life's door. We will not have to wait for peace of mind; it will be waiting for us.

What is surrender-light
If not giving God
Your earthly all
And Heavenly all?

My past was completely destroyed on the day I employed my surrendering thoughts to help me reach my God.

We become the lamb of God when we offer ourselves unconditionally to God's Will, and when God unconditionally and constantly makes us feel that we are not only His chosen instruments, but also His eternal friends. Him to realise, Him to fulfil and Him to manifest on earth: for this we came into the world. When we entered into the world, God offered us His inner Promise to unveil our Reality and manifest our Divinity. And when we go back to Heaven, God shall tell us that we have played our role, we have fulfilled His Promise here on earth.

A spiritual seeker
Does not have to travel
On many roads.
He only has to run
On one road:
The road of surrender.

Your aspiration for God-realisation and your surrender to God's Will kill all your fear, born and yet to be born.

When God's Will becomes our will, when we offer to God not only the possessions and achievements of the outer world, but also the awareness, the aspiration and the realisation of the inner world, then we become the lion of God. When we do not aspire, God in us is a sleeping lion. When we aspire, pray and meditate, God in us becomes a roaring lion. This roaring lion devours our teeming darkness and ignorance.

Soon to be announced:
My vital has cheerfully
And unconditionally surrendered
To God's all-loving Heart
And all-illumining Eye.

The most glorious beginning of my miracle-life: I have started loving God, my Beloved Supreme, in His own Way.

The absolutely best way of making progress is by constantly praying to the Supreme to fulfil Himself in His own Way through you. There is nothing wrong with praying to the Supreme for peace, light and bliss, or for anything else that is really good. But if you want to go beyond that, then you will pray, "Please fulfil Yourself in and through me in Your own Way." That is absolutely the best way to make progress. But if you can not do that all the time, then do the second best thing, which is to pray for peace, light, bliss and other divine qualities which will eventually take you to Him and enable you to please Him in His own Way.

Mine is not the way
To follow the world.
Mine is not the way
To lead the world.
Mine is the way
To walk along with God.

Unconditional surrender comes only when the mind has become totally one with the soul.

Who says that you do not know the Will of the Supreme? Is there anybody who does not know the Will of the Supreme? No. If you remain in the heart, then at every moment you will know what God's Will is. But if you remain in the mind, never, never will you be able to know the Will of the Supreme. You may get grandiose thoughts and lofty ideas, but they will not be the Will of the Supreme. Life's victory or defeat, life's acceptance or rejection, are not the ultimate Reality in the Eyes of the Supreme. He laughs at our acceptance or rejection of a thing, at our victories and defeats. But He triumphantly smiles at us when His Will becomes our will. We do not have to become great in the outer world to prove to the world or to Him that we are worthy instruments of His. Never does He care for our earthly status. He cares only for one thing: our constant oneness with His Will.

God loves me.
He loves my helpless heart
More.
He loves my surrender-life
Most.

The soul in me is for God's constant use. The body in me is for God's constant use. My very life is for God's constant use.

When an aspirant is totally surrendered to God's Will, he will get abundant joy. He will feel all joy in his heart and he will live in constant joy. He will not be able to account for it or give any meaning to it. Early in the morning when he first gets up, he will get a very sweet feeling or sensation. If he touches a wall, he will get joy; if he touches a mirror, he will also get joy. His own joy enters into everything he sees. At times he may see that a solid wall is full of joy; a tree will be full of joy. If a taxi-cab goes by, he will see intense joy in the driver, even in the car itself. His inner joy will enter into each person, each object; and it will pervade everything.

Your surrender-acceptance
Of God's Will
Has created a new hope
For the entire world.

Inner surrender transforms life into an infinite progress. It gives life the soulful assurance that life lives in God and God alone.

When we walk along the path of spirituality, at every moment we try to listen to the dictates of our inner being. The more we listen to our inner being, the greater is our joy and the higher our fulfilment. And then, when our term is over, when we have to enter into another world for a short rest, we also surrender. To whom? To the Inner Pilot, the Lord Supreme. At the end of our journey, we surrender our very breath to the Supreme. Then we again get joy, perfect joy, unalloyed joy.

I surrender to the Supreme
Not because I feel I am helpless,
But because I feel
His Oneness-Delight is something
I have all along been craving
In my own life.

We have to establish our conscious oneness with God. Then there is no surrender. It is only mutual give and take.

There are millions and millions of people on earth who are not conscious of the fact that they are the instruments of God. Just because we have accepted the spiritual life, we are fully conscious of the fact that we are the instruments and God is the Player. If we can maintain that kind of feeling, there will be no temptation. As long as we want to be the doers, wrong forces will come to attack us and devour us. But if we become absolutely helpless and feel, "I am the instrument, O God. You play. You utilise me," then all temptation will come and attack our Inner Pilot, God, and He will not be affected at all.

Whoever experiences
His life's surrender-smiles
As a permanent reality
Is undoubtedly the choicest instrument
Of his Beloved Supreme

When the aspirant bitterly starves his questioning mind and feeds his surrender sumptuously, God says: "The time is ripe. I come."

Human love binds; divine love expands. Human devotion is our unconscious attachment; divine devotion is our conscious awareness of our ultimate reality. Human surrender is the surrender of a slave to his master; divine surrender is the surrender of the finite to the Infinite. This surrender is conscious, wholehearted and unconditional, and it allows the human being to realise his Source, God.

In the morning
I wish to be perfected
Through my blossoming faith.
In the evening
I wish to be perfected
Through my surrendering life.

November

Service

Choose to serve. The world will start loving you immediately.

A spiritual person has found his work. His work is selfless service. His work is dedicated action. Indeed, he has no need of any other blessedness. His action is the divine acceptance of earthly existence. And for this he needs a perfect body, a strong mind, a soulful heart and a supremely inspired life of inner receptivity and outer capacity.

Yesterday I desired to achieve
So that I could become
Something or someone great
In the world.
Today my desire has been purified
And transformed into my aspiration
To serve the world.

NOVEMBER 2

To serve God, I wish my life to be a life of selfless donation.

Do you want your life to be of service to God so that you can fulfil His mission? If so, then here and now give the soul back its throne. You have driven the soul away and placed the ego on its throne. Do cordially welcome the soul and unite yourself with it. At that time, fear leaves you, ignorance leaves you; finally death leaves you. Eternity welcomes you, Infinity welcomes you; finally, Immortality welcomes you.

Do you want to shine?
You can easily shine
Like the sun
In your self-offering
To God in man.

NOVEMBER 3

God teaches me how to serve Him in humanity.

Why do we work? We work to support ourselves, to support our dear ones. We may also work to keep our bodies in perfect condition. But a true aspirant looks upon work differently. He sees work as a veritable blessing. To him, each difficult and apparently painful job is a blessing in disguise. To him, work is nothing short of a dedicated service. He has discovered the truth that by offering the results of what he says, does and thinks, he will be able to realise God. He works for the sake of God. He lives for the sake of God. He realises Divinity for the sake of God.

In Heaven
The souls are placed
According to their self-giving,
Man-serving
And God-loving deeds
Performed here on earth.

Reveal constantly what you are: a supremely chosen instrument of God.

While you are doing your daily activities you should pray to the Supreme, to the Inner Pilot, who is operating in and through you. God has infinite Concern for human beings in each of their activities. If you are not concerned, that is a mistake. You will have concern, but you will not feel that this concern is coming from you. Feel that it is coming from somewhere else and that an Inner Hand is guiding you. This is the right approach.

> *When you are ready to tell God*
> *That you have the willingness,*
> *God will say to you:*
> *"Lo, My child, I am here*
> *With My Fruitfulness for you."*

When I am all devotion to service-light, I am with the active and for the active.

When we talk and talk, we enter consciously and deliberately into the domain of ignorance. When we talk and act, at times we see a yawning gulf between our speech and our action. We say something and we do something totally different. We make a solemn promise to do something, but when reality dawns we see a vast gulf between our promise and its fulfillment. But when we act spontaneously, soulfully and unconditionally—when we offer our dedicated service—an unseen Hand guides us, shapes us and moulds us into the very image of our Inner Pilot. It is only by devotedly serving the Inner Pilot in each individual that we can make our life meaningful and fruitful.

> *If you want to become a lion-leader*
> *To roar and manifest God,*
> *Then at this very moment*
> *Turn yourself into a lamb-slave of man,*
> *The evolving God.*

Real selfless service is that which does not expect a favourable result.

Selfless service is only for the sake of self-giving; the result will come naturally. If there is an action, there will be a reaction. But the action will be performed not to please ourselves in our own way, but to please God in His own Way. We shall act when we are inspired from within. We shall work soulfully and consciously. If we work without inspiration, then we are working mechanically, like workers in a factory who do not want to be there. We have become another machine. Selfless service is not like that. It is cheerful, soulful, conscious and constant. First it is soulful service; then it is selfless; and finally, when it becomes unconditional and uncaring for the result, then it becomes perfect selfless service.

He is extremely happy
Because he has become
The marriage of his heart's love
And his life's service.

Two lives: human life and divine life. Human life cries to live; divine life lives to offer.

When we use the term selfless service, we cannot and we must not expect anything. If it is devoted service, we can expect some reward; but when it becomes selfless, then we cannot expect any reward. When we are able to do real selfless service with no desire or expectation of reward, the result we shall get will be far beyond all our expectations. Also, during the performance of real selfless service, we get abundant joy. We do not have to wait for any result or after-effect. Selfless service itself is the greatest joy and highest reward.

Love!
You will know
What the human life is all about.
Serve!
You will know
What the divine life is all about.

The ego in me helps humanity. The soul in me serves humanity. The God in me is fed by humanity when I realise that everybody around me is none other than God Himself.

The easiest way to kindle the flame of your aspiration is through dedicated selfless service. This selfless service has to be constant and spontaneous. When you are doing something for yourself or for someone else, you have to feel that you are serving the Supreme.

Do you want
To deserve God's Love?
Then serve God the man
In God's unfinished Creation.

When you are doing something for yourself, you have to feel that you are serving the better part, the higher part, the nobler part, the more fulfilling part, the more illumining part inside you. At each moment you have to feel that you are a dedicated server. In this way, your flame of inspiration will go higher.

Who aspires? He who feels that there is something higher, deeper, vaster, more profound than what he has right now. Who serves? If you say that the inferior serves the superior, that is only true in the outer world. A slave or a servant, you may say, serves the master because the master is superior. That may be true in the ordinary human world. But in the inner world we see a different thing. We see that the aspirant is serving his own best part inside himself. He is trying to serve the highest portion within himself.

If you give from your heart,
Then your offering will be
Not only unimaginable
But also indisputable.

I serve God not because He is infinitely greater than I, but because He is my Eternity's beloved Friend, my Beloved Supreme and my Eternity's All.

When you, as an aspirant, serve your highest, your best part, it is not only for the sake of inner peace, light and bliss, but it is in order to become totally one with that highest part. The earthly servant's role is over when he gets his money. He never dares to think of becoming the master one day. It is beyond his imagination. But when you are serving your highest part as an aspirant, you have to feel at every moment that you are growing into that highest part inside you and that you will ultimately become consciously one with your own highest part.

Human nature
Does not change
And cannot change
Without selfless service.

The Golden Shore of the Beyond will always remain a far cry unless and until we not only believe in the supreme secret of self-giving but also practise it at every moment.

In every way—through thought, through action, through your own service, mentally, vitally and physically—you have to feel that you are an object of dedication to be used by God and by God's children. If you can feel at every moment that you are ready to serve the aspiring ones, the ones who are seated in the same boat as you are, in the Boat of the Supreme, only then will you be able to feel that your aspiration-flame is at every moment burning bright, brighter, brightest.

Every morning I must realise
That I have the golden opportunity
Of an unused day before me
To use in a divine way.

A life on earth is not meant for pleasure; a life on earth is meant for self-offering. Self-offering eventually makes us what God is.

When you really have something to offer to the world, then you can become truly humble. A tree, when it has no fruit to offer, remains erect. But when the tree is laden with fruit, it bends down. When you have genuine humility, it is a sign that you have something to offer mankind. If you are all pride and ego, then nobody will be able to get anything worthwhile from you.

If your service-life
Is only increasing your ego-power,
Then rest assured
You are a stark failure
In the inner world.

Let us serve the world soulfully. The pay we receive for our service will be in the currency of gratitude, God's Gratitude. God is the only gratitude.

While we are constantly achieving something, we have to remember to be humble in order to be of greater service to mankind. But first we have to know that if we want to become humble, it is certainly because we want to become happy. And in self-giving we become really happy. Real humility is the expansion of our consciousness and our service.

When I do selfless service
An hour every day,
God tells me
That I am His dear friend,
Very dear friend.

Forget about all the unhappy experiences that you have given and received. Think only of how you can give joy to others and thus make yourself happy.

Before our realisation, when we do not know our Self, our problem is smaller. But when we discover our Self, when we understand our Self, when we know our Self, when we realise our highest Self, at that time the real problem starts: how shall we help mankind? At that time, if it is God's Will, we have to give, whether mankind accepts our offering or not.

How I wish my heart
To remain always
Under the control of my soul,
So that every day my inspiration
Can soar beyond my belief,
And never will my service-offering
Become mechanical.

Happiness is in our self-giving. We give what we are. What we are is our aspiration, inner cry, and what we give is our dedication-life. It is in self-giving that we grow into God. Self-giving is the precursor of God-becoming.

There is no such thing as sacrifice. What we call sacrifice is really a constant self-giving based on one's awareness of universal oneness, and a constant heroic dynamism which enables one to conquer ignorance-sea in the battlefield of life and transform it into a sea of wisdom-light. If one can do this, then in this lifetime one will be able to realise God and become perfect.

Give what you have
And what you are.
Then you will be blessed
With new mornings
In new worlds.

The gift of my outer life to my inner life is my constantly soulful service.

You can establish your perfect oneness with the Supreme by constant self-giving and also by not expecting anything in your own way from the Supreme. Expect everything from Him in His own Way. He will give you at His choice Hour what He wants to give you. On your part there should be no expectation, whether He gives you a penny or one thousand dollars, whether He is giving you an iota of light or whether He floods your entire being with light. Let Him give you what He wants to give you in His own Way, at His own Hour. In that way only can you establish your perfect oneness with the Supreme.

Selfless service
Is man's visible love for God
In God-manifestation on earth.

NOVEMBER 17

I need an unconditionally self-giving life.

While you are working with your spiritual brothers and sisters, please feel that they are equally important in the eye of the Supreme, in the eye of your Master, in the eye of your soul. You have two eyes, and you feel that both are equally important. You do not feel that the left eye is more important than the right eye, or vice versa. When you have two things which you claim as your very own, you try to be impartial. You do not identify yourself with your thumb and criticise your little finger. No! Whatever capacity your little finger has comes from God, and whatever capacity your thumb has also comes from God. Ego comes when the feeling of oneness is missing or when you want to show your capacity to others. If you separate your little finger from your thumb, at that time ego comes into play. If you do not make this separation, you will say that everything and everyone is good in God's Eye.

We can arrive at perfection's gate
Only when we work together
Lovingly, untiringly and selflessly.

NOVEMBER 18

An act of self-offering is one step more towards God-becoming.

To perfect our actions we have to feel that we are not the doer, that the Supreme is the only doer. We have to feel that the inspiration for the action is not ours, and the fruit of the action is not ours. If we can feel that we are just the instruments of the Supreme, our actions can be perfect.

If you think that you are
Most graciously helping others,
You are badly mistaken.
You should feel that you are offering
Your service-smile
To the Supreme in others.

If you are consciously and devotedly doing everything that you are supposed to do—prayer, meditation, selfless service—and at the same time if you are not expecting anything either from the Supreme or from yourself, then you can have no regret.

Personal effort is of paramount importance. Unless and until we give to the world at large what we have and what we are, we cannot grow into the all-widening and all-embracing Reality which we call the Universal Consciousness of the Transcendental Height. This personal effort is also founded upon the unconditional Compassion of the Supreme. What we call effort in reality is a result of the Supreme's Grace, which rains constantly on our devoted head and our surrendered heart.

Just do one thing
Correctly and selflessly every day.
Then you are bound to see and feel
That God will do everything for you
Not only sleeplessly
But also unconditionally.

For progress, be conscious and self-giving.

When we give we become infinitely more. A tiny drop gives its reality, its existence, to the mighty ocean. It gives only a tiny drop. But when it gives wholeheartedly, when it surrenders its separate existence, it becomes one with the ocean itself. What we give, in return we get infinitely more. Self-giving is God-becoming. The moment we give ourselves soulfully, devotedly, unreservedly and unconditionally, we become the Infinite, as a tiny drop offers itself to the ocean and becomes the ocean. When we offer our little earthly existence to our Beloved Supreme, we become immediately and inseparably one with His Universal and Transcendental Reality.

> *To be a God-dreamer*
> *What you need*
> *Is a God-lover's heart*
> *And a man-server's life.*

When we go deep, very deep into the inmost recesses of our soul, we feel there is no such thing as sacrifice.

Each time you do something you can feel that this action is nothing but an expression of love. Offering love through thought and action right now is of supreme importance in your life. While thinking and while acting if you can feel that you are offering love to mankind, to the rest of the world, then you can be more receptive to the universal Love which is all for you.

> *Satisfaction-pension*
> *Will always be there*
> *For those who have offered*
> *Their aspiration-services*
> *Soulfully and unreservedly*
> *To God,*
> *Their beloved Employer.*

"Give unconditionally." This is the meaning of God. "Receive cheerfully." This is the meaning of man.

Before we do something, before we say something, before we become something, we have to ask our inner being. We have to go deep within and ask our soul whether it is God's Will, whether God wants it to be done. At every moment we have to ask whether God wants it or not. Otherwise there are many ways in which you can please me and I can please you on the basis of our own mental understanding. Giving is a very good thing; receiving is a very good thing. But again, it is God who is supposed to inspire us to give and to receive. Action can be done without asking God's Wisdom, but if we beg of God's Wisdom to guide us and then we act, then it is God's responsibility.

God places
His Heart's Nectar-Crown
Upon the seeker's
Selfless service-head.

It is never too late to become a good instrument of God.

Love is wisdom, but inside this love we have to feel God's Presence first. If we feel God's Presence in each action, then automatically it becomes wisdom because God is all wisdom. So before we say anything, we need approval. If we do not get approval, then we shall remain silent. Our direction we will get from within. God will not remain silent; He will not be indifferent. God does not remain silent, only we do not go deep within in order to hear His Voice, His Dictates. He is not like an indifferent human being whom we ask again and again without getting any answer. Go deep within. Immediately God will answer either yes or no.

God is now setting
Not only new
But also high standards
For those who want to love Him
And serve Him
In His own Way.

It is never too late for me to serve my Beloved Supreme inside my brothers and sisters: mankind.

Humility we have to take as a divine gift and a supreme gift. It is something that we have to offer to mankind. We have to feel that humility is our feeling of consecrated oneness with humanity. If we take humility in the highest and purest sense of the term, then we can become really humble. Humility is not a matter of touching the feet of somebody, no. It is something that has to be shared with the rest of the world. It is the God-life within us. The higher we go, the greater is our promise to the Supreme in mankind. The more light we receive by virtue of our humility, the more we have to offer to mankind.

My loving heart
Has a message for me:
God is always for me.

My serving life
Has a message for me:
I am always for God.

Give the world a moment of your concern. God will always listen to your heart's prayer.

We have to know that there is only one way to become humble and that is to see what happens to an individual when he sees, achieves and grows into the light. Does he keep it all for himself? No. He shares with the rest of the world. And when he shares, the world is nourished, the world is fulfilled.

Peace you get
Only by helping others
To become peaceful.
Bliss you get
Only by helping others
To become soulful.

God's Secrets are only for those who are God-servers in man.

If we, as human beings, want to be transformed into divine beings, we have to see and feel the necessity of divine sacrifice on earth. Now, how are we going to know if this sacrifice of ours is complete? We can know that it is complete the moment we feel that by giving we are not only getting more, but becoming complete. Sacrifice takes the form of love. The mother gives to her child all that she has, wholeheartedly. When we give a little peace or joy to others and we feel that we still have more inside us, then we have to feel that we have not made the other person complete and at the same time we have not made ourselves complete. When we offer our peace, love and bliss to another person fully and wholeheartedly, then only can our vessel be filled to the brim. God Himself will fill it for us.

Selfless service
Keeps your faith in God
Sweeter than the sweetest
And makes your oneness-love
With God
Stronger than the strongest.

If your heart is truly bleeding for humanity's need, how can you have insecurity's ugly face?

To help others in order to feed your own ego is useless. You have to know that it is a serious mistake, and that it will delay your progress. So the best thing is to see if you are getting an inner command to help others. If you feel that you do have an inner command to work in this way, then the next thing on your part is to do it devotedly. You should be grateful to the Inner Pilot for authorizing you to serve Him in this way. But if you are not getting a command from an inner, higher source, then you have to know that your actions are being motivated by your ego; in that case, you should stop.

In your life of service to humanity
Confidence is supremely good,
But do not develop
Disproportionate self-confidence,
Not to speak of pride and haughtiness.

How can God ever deny a truth-loving and world-serving soul? Impossible!

While helping others you have to feel that the help that you are giving is not coming from you. It is not you who is helping, guiding or moulding a particular person; it is your Inner Pilot. You have to become a mere channel. While touching someone or while talking to someone, feel that you are just the channel.

My Lord,
May the unreservedly devoted season
Of self-giving
Be mine,
And may the surprisingly pleased season
Of receiving
Be Yours.

Every day you must shed tears for this poor earth if you really care for God the man.

Suppose that you do not know what the truth is, but you have aspiration and sincere concern for someone. You want to help him, but you do not know what you are going to say. At that time, do not form any idea of how to help him, or what you will tell him or how you are going to approach the truth. Make your mind an empty vessel. Then let the vessel be filled with God's Light and Wisdom, and just share it with him. How can you do this? You can do it only through your constant surrender.

If you do not limit
Your service-life,
God will not stop
His manifestation-march
In you.

Selfless service is man's visible love for God in God-manifestation on earth.

It is through constant self-giving that you can march towards your self-perfection. There is no other way. Give yourself to the Supreme soulfully, devotedly and unconditionally, and feel that there is nothing that He will not do for you. And again, even if He does not do anything for you, it is His business. He knows what is best for you. What you think you need is not the right thing. What He thinks you need is the right thing. Your self-giving is absolutely the right thing, because this is the one thing in your life that the Supreme wants from you. So only through self-giving can you march towards perfection.

If you love man in God,
The adventure of consciousness-light
Will embrace you without fail.
If you serve God in man,
The consciousness-light of adventure
Will claim you and treasure you.

December

Manifestation

DECEMBER 1

The secret of manifestation is dedication in secret.

If somebody asks us, "What have you done for God?" what will our answer be? We can be filled with pride when we say, "God has done this for me, God has done that for me, God has done everything for me." But if somebody asks us, "What have you done for God?" what will be our answer? Silence! So the little personal effort that we make is for our own good. When we make this personal effort, our whole life is surcharged with divine pride. It is not our ego, but our conscious oneness with God that prompts us to do something for our Dearest. If we sincerely make personal efforts, God is bound to be thrilled with us. Why? Because He can tell the world, "My child, My chosen instrument, has done this for Me and that for Me." Through personal effort we can make our existence on earth worthy and, at the same time, we can make God proud of us.

If you are
A real human being,
Then you will have
Only one answer to God:
A cheerful YES!

DECEMBER 2

God has given us capacity. According to our capacity He demands manifestation of us. Manifestation beyond our capacity God has never demanded and will never demand.

We do not have to know what God wants us to manifest. Only we have to pray to God every day: "O Beloved Supreme, do manifest Yourself in and through me. I do not know and do not need to know what You want from me. My fervent wish, my fervent aspiration, is only that You will manifest Yourself in and through me, that You will make me an unconditionally surrendered God-lover and instrument of Yours.

> *My Beloved Supreme tells me*
> *That my smiling dreams*
> *Have to be transformed*
> *Into my dancing realities.*
> *Then only will I be able*
> *To please Him*
> *In His own Way.*

A realised soul cries for God-manifestation. He feels that once he is realised, his role in the Cosmic Drama has properly begun.

We only have to cry sincerely to God to manifest Himself in and through us. If we become an unconditional instrument, what will God do? He will fulfil Himself in and through us in His own Way. So let us express our wish to manifest God not by asking, "God, tell me what You want me to do; then I will be able to please You," but by saying, "God, do what You want in and through me."

When your mind starts enjoying
Complete union with God,
Your life, without fail, will become
The absolute manifestation of God.

DECEMBER 4

My inner experience is God's continuous manifestation of His own Perfection in and through me.

What is perfection? Perfection is realisation. Perfection is manifestation. Perfection in the inner world means realisation. Perfection in the outer world means manifestation. A seeker is a fusion of individuality and personality. When a seeker carries his selfless individuality into the highest vision of Reality and offers his all-loving personality to the Absolute Beyond, he achieves perfection in the world of Infinity's Eternity.

When God came and told me
That He would make me
A perfect instrument of His,
I shared this good news
With my heart
Immediately.

DECEMBER 5

When I smile, God is my manifesting experience.

It is true that if you have peace or light, then you can manifest God. But instead of praying for these divine qualities, it is better to pray to God to give you what He feels you need most for your inner evolution and His fulfilment. It is good to feel, "God, if You do not want me to be Your perfect instrument, no harm. Somebody else can be, if that is Your Will. If You want to make even my worst possible enemy Your best instrument, do make him. I only want You to be fulfilled in Your own Way." If you can sincerely offer that kind of prayer to God, then your problems are solved.

Forget all and start again!
Muster the courage
To become a perfect instrument
Of God.

DECEMBER 6

**If God wants you, open your eyes, close your ears
and run.**

We have to feel that action itself is a great blessing,
but the result of action we have to take as an experience. According to our own limited understanding,
we see it as either failure or success. But in God's Eye,
failure and success are both just experiences which
help to develop our consciousness. When acting we
have to expect only the fulfilment of God's Will.
Whatever happens we should see as the experience
that God wanted to give us. Today, He may give us
the experience of failure. Tomorrow, He may give us
another experience which will satisfy us outwardly.
But if we live a spiritual life, no matter what result
comes to us from our action, we shall be satisfied.

Don't discuss,
Don't think,
Just do!

God will never ask us to do anything beyond our capacity. He has given us the necessary capacity.

You may say that you do not know where the goal is right now. No harm. Just move. If you go in the wrong direction, soon you will realise it and go in another direction. Eventually you will reach your goal. But if you do not move at all, there is absolutely no hope that you will go in the right direction. If you cannot do disinterested work, selfless work, then work with a motive first. If ego and vanity come in while you are helping someone, let them come. A day will dawn when you will feel that the satisfaction that you are getting is not enough. You will realise it does not last more than a few seconds. Then you will try to work in a more divine way.

Who am I?
I am my life's
Unfinished God-work.

We shall not fail God because we love God and because God loves us. Love is oneness, inseparable oneness. When we sing the song of inseparable oneness, we cannot fail.

We and God must have reciprocal faith. Our faith in God will make us His chosen instruments. His faith in us will inspire us to manifest Him totally, unreservedly and perfectly here on earth. Our faith in Him will give us what we desperately need—realisation. His faith in us will give Him the opportunity to manifest Himself in and through us. We need Him for our highest realisation; He, out of His infinite Kindness, needs us for His divine manifestation.

My God-manifestation-promise
Will never be broken by me.
My God-satisfaction-hope
Will ever be spoken by me.

When God sends for you, be determined to be available at your heart-home.

Ultimately, personal effort has to grow into a dynamic self-surrender. When we do something, we offer at the Feet of God the result of our action along with the aspiration that we have used to do that particular thing. When the results and the aspiration, the inner urge, we can offer to God, this is called true surrender. But just to lie at God's Feet like a corpse and let God work in us, through us and for us is wrong. God does not want to work in and through a dead body. He wants someone who is aspiring, someone who wants to be energised and who wants to do something for Him. He wants someone who is active and dynamic and who wants to manifest all the divine qualities here on earth.

No more, no more I need
A paralysis-life.
I need a life
Of quick accomplishment.

Each moment you can utilise for God, for the Supreme, or for your own purpose. The time that is passing by is not going to come back.

Duty is painful, tedious and monotonous simply because we do it with our ego, pride and vanity. Duty is pleasant, encouraging and inspiring when we do it for God's sake. What we need is to change our attitude towards duty. If we work for the sake of God, then there is no duty. All is joy. All is beauty. Each action has to be performed and offered at the Feet of God. Duty for God's sake is the duty supreme. No right have we to undertake any other duty before we work out our own spiritual salvation. Did God not entrust us with this wonderful task at the time of our very birth? The supreme duty is to constantly strive for God-realisation. Time is short, but our soul's mission on earth is lofty. How can we waste time? Why should we spend time in the pleasures of the senses?

When God reveals
His Plans,
Show your immediate eagerness
To manifest Him.

If you do not put your meditation into action, then you will be running with only one leg.

Many have realised the Highest, the Transcendental Truth. But there are few who cry for the perfection of humanity. There are very few who try to change the face of the world. The chosen instruments of God want to manifest God here on earth. They do not care much for earthly good or evil. They transcend the so-called good and evil. They care only for God's inner Dictates. Constantly they listen to the Dictates of their Inner Pilot; and then, on the strength of their inseparable oneness with their Inner Pilot, they offer their selfless, dedicated service to humanity. They try to offer knowledge, divine knowledge, to aspiring humanity. Again, they tell humanity that God-realisation is not their sole monopoly.

I need only my heart's happiness
To cry sleeplessly
For God-manifestation
Here on earth.

In God's Cosmic Play, each individual soul takes a God-revealing and God-manifesting part.

We have to enter into the domain of manifestation. If we do not manifest what we have realised here on earth, if Mother Earth does not receive the fruit of our realisation, and if She does not have it for good, we can never be truly fulfilled. Mother Earth has to be fed with the fruit of our realisation. Here on earth, the manifestation of realisation has to take place; and when manifestation takes place, perfection is bound to dawn. Perfect Perfection is nothing other than the absolute manifestation of God's Transcendental Will here on earth.

I may not be or cannot be a member
Of God's Vision-manifestation-team
On earth,
But I dearly love the team's
God-oneness-heart
And profoundly admire
Its God-fulness-hands.
But I do know and I do feel
That God will eventually make me
A member of His Vision-manifestation-team.

In the spiritual life, a qualified and God-manifesting instrument is he who at once learns the instructions given by the Inner Pilot and unlearns the instructions offered by ignorance-night.

You can best feel that you are an instrument of the Supreme if you can feel that there is no other reality but the Supreme. This is the first step. Then you have to feel that you can live without God, you can live without yourself, but God cannot live without you.

You have tried.
You have not succeeded.
That does not mean
That you will not try anymore.
Try once more!
You will not only succeed
In the life that becomes
But also proceed
In the life that eternally is.

DECEMBER 14

We are crying only for one thing: to become good, perfect, unconditional instruments of God so that God can manifest Himself in and through us.

If you can make yourself feel that you are needed by God, whether you need God or not, then your problem is solved. It is not your human ego that is saying, "I am very great. I do not need God, but God needs me." No. Just because God has so much more knowledge and wisdom, He needs you. Just because He is the Creator, He is conscious of His Creation.

Keep doing the right things.
God Himself will go
And collect the gratitude-buds
That the world owes you.

Do not take your Lord Supreme for granted. When you go to the other world, you may not be able to see Him at your sweet will if you have not sincerely tried to satisfy Him during the years and years He offered you countless opportunities on earth.

When my heart's only cry is to please God in His own Way, then God can manifest Himself in and through me. When my inner cry carries me to God, I say to Him, "O my Beloved Supreme, make me Your perfect instrument." When God comes to me, He gives me a broad Smile—a wide, soulful, illumining Smile—and says, "My child, I shall make you My perfect instrument and, at the same time, I will manifest Myself in and through you."

There was a time
When I died
For the perfection of man.
Now I am living only
For the manifestation of God.

God wants each human being to be an unlimited supply of inner capacity.

God shows us what work we must do if we can soulfully promise to Him that our work will be nothing but an extension of His divine manifestation. Then He is bound to show us our work. But if our work is an expansion of our ego, God does not recognise us. At that time we are nothing but strangers to Him.

An unexpected visitor
Entered into his heart
To tell him that the Heavenly God
Does not mind if he fails
So long as he wants to try
Again and again.

How far is God's perfect manifestation? As far as man's total transformation and his unconditional surrender.

He who aspires enters into beauty: beauty that makes his life fruitful in the highest realm of consciousness and meaningful here in the field of manifestation. The beauty that we see around us, we can utilise to go deep within. The beauty that we feel and embody, we can use to perfect God's outer Creation.

If you wait for the approval
Of your friends
In everything that you do,
You are not going to succeed
At all
In this lifetime
In anything.

I shall become a devoted, faithful, soulful, unreserved and unconditional instrument of my Beloved Supreme.

To see the Beyond, what is absolutely necessary is our certainty—our implicit faith in ourselves. We have to feel that we are God's chosen children. We have to feel that we embody infinite Light, infinite Truth and infinite Bliss and that now we have to reveal and manifest these divine qualities. Revelation and manifestation are absolutely necessary. The moment we start revealing and manifesting our inner divinity, we will see that we already embody infinite Truth, infinite Light and all the other divine qualities of the Supreme.

Look around!
You will see so many things
To do for the world.

Dive deep within!
You will not only see
But also at once do
Many things for God.

If your Lord Supreme requests you to do something, rest assured, He has already given you the capacity—even more than necessary—long before you actually need it.

Reality sees that when it wants to manifest itself on earth, it is human will-power which takes up the challenge to help. Man's other divine qualities hesitate; when reality wants to manifest through them, they feel that the time is not ripe. They say, "We are preparing ourselves. Please give us a little more time." But when reality comes to will-power, reality feels tremendous joy and delight because reality sees that human will-power is ready to place it on its shoulders and carry it all around.

What else
Is my tremendous achievement,
O my Lord Supreme,
If not the manifestation
Of Your own supremely unparalleled
Compassion-Capacity?

Do you really love God? If so, then speak like God compassionately, and act like God unconditionally.

The Beyond is in the Eternal Now. If we can dare to feel that we are God's chosen children, then we can without fail live in the Beyond. We have to feel that we are everything and that in us is everything. God is within us; God is without us. We must know that our human existence is meaningful only when we become a perfect channel for the Divine to manifest the Ultimate Truth on earth.

Becoming a perfect instrument
Of God
Is so difficult
Because giving up
Is so easy.

My soul's promise and my life of love, devotion and surrender will fulfil our Beloved Supreme throughout the length and breadth of the world.

To offer ourselves as a perfect flower to God, first we have to become the flower itself. How do we become a flower? We become a flower through constant remembrance of what we are going to eventually be. We are going to be God's instrument. Now if we are an instrument, it means that we are not the doer; somebody else is the doer. We are not the creator; we are not the creation; we are not even the observer. We are only an experience that God is having. God is having an experience in us, with us and for us. When we feel that God is the Creator, the Experience and the Observer in us, that we are not doing anything, but that it is He who is doing everything in and through and for us, at that time we become a perfect flower to be offered to the Supreme.

Get your aspiration-heart
In perfect tune with God
Before you begin the concert
Of your manifestation-light.

Do not be in a hurry. God will definitely lengthen your time if it is needed for you to please Him in His own Way.

The Supreme's perfect warriors are those souls who have realised God and are now manifesting Him on earth, souls who have made a conscious promise to struggle for the Supreme and fight against ignorance, to enter into the world and perfect it. These souls are fulfilling the request of the Supreme to come to earth. They come down and see all the souls swimming in the sea of ignorance and lift these souls into the sea of light.

If you are already an awakened soul,
Then you must realise
That God has already given you
A supreme task to perform:
He wants you to work
For His Vision's world-blossoms.

No good heart will ever shirk any challenge, for a good heart is braver than the bravest when it has to manifest its Beloved Supreme on earth.

Once divinity, reality or any divine qualities are properly manifested, then they are permanent. They become part and parcel of Mother Earth. They become the possession of humanity's aspiration. So the God-realised seeker tries to manifest. And when he manifests, he feels his complete oneness with the Absolute Pilot. He becomes the perfect instrument of divinity's perfection. Being a perfect instrument of his Beloved Supreme, the seeker tries to manifest the divinity which he has been entrusted with.

The beauty of a sweet hope
Has to be transformed
Into the duty of a powerful promise,
And the promise has to be manifested
As the divinity of an infallible fulfilment.

DECEMBER 24

Hold fast to your life's obedience-tree if you really want a real God-manifestation-life.

Real spiritual life means carrying our Beloved Supreme inside our heart. When you go to the office, when you go to the supermarket, you can carry the Supreme inside your heart and inside your mind. At every moment you can try to manifest the Supreme.

Work by itself proves nothing.
Work for mankind proves something
Always appreciable.
Work for God is something always adorable,
Also profitable.

If you wear your heart's oneness-uniform, then God will inform the world that you are His choicest instrument.

You can manifest the Supreme in many different activities, but you have to surrender to His Will. God wants you, like me, to manifest Him through a life of action. Each time you get a thought, are you offering it to the Supreme? If the answer is yes, then you are doing the right thing. Whether it is a bad, undivine thought or a good, divine thought, if you can offer it to the Supreme, then you are doing the right thing.

When my prayer is an action,
My earth's separation-division-life
Disappears
And my Heaven's oneness-multiplication-life
Appears.

DECEMBER 26

God has given you an imaginative mind. Can you not offer Him a creative life?

Our life of manifestation and our life of aspiration are inseparable. Early in the morning you meditate. This is your life of aspiration. But you can not remain inside your room. For twenty-four hours it is not possible for you to remain inside your room. If you do not go to work, then you can not earn money to buy food and support yourself. If you stay only with aspiration and meditate, meditate, remaining always closeted, then who is going to bring you food and support you? You have to support yourself. Aspiration you have done: now go outside for manifestation. Aspiration and manifestation cannot be separated.

If you want to satisfy
Any wish of yours,
Then keep in mind
Your ancient promise:
God-manifestation will be
Your life-breath.

I go to God with my heart's inner delight. My only cry is to please Him in His own Way. God comes to me with a broad smile, for now He can manifest Himself in and through me.

World problems can be solved only when we consciously remind ourselves of our soul's promise to God before we entered into the world arena. This Creation of God's we have to accept as our field of experience, as our field of experiment, as our field of God-revelation and God-manifestation. Each individual soul makes the solemn promise to God to see God in God's own Way, to fulfil God in God's own Way before it assumes its earthly cloak. But the ignorance of the world veils the light of the soul. This experience of the soul is an unfortunate incident in the soul's life, but it does not last forever. God's infinite Compassion from above and man's inner urge meet together and the soul again comes to the fore, offers its light to the world of obscurity and fulfils the promise that it made to the Absolute Supreme.

God compassionately asks me,
"Will you be available?"
He never asks me,
"Will you be able?"

DECEMBER 28

Inside my God-hungry heart I always keep a sweet, soulful and beautiful God-manifestation-dream.

When I have more peace in my mind, more joy in my heart, more soulfulness in my vital, more selflessness in my body, more determination in my aspiration, more perfection in my dedication, more Compassion from God and more cooperation from humanity, at that time I shall become a most perfect instrument of God in the inner world and a most perfect representative of mankind in the outer world.

If you have a seeker's heart,
Then at the very mention
Of your Lord Supreme,
Your eyes of indifference
To the outer world of manifestation
Will be transformed into
A heart of sleepless concern.

Siddhartha Becomes the Buddha

The combination of profound insight and simplicity of language makes this book an excellent choice for anyone, young or old, seeking to understand one of the world's most influential spiritual figures. $6.95

Music by Sri Chinmoy

Flute Music for Meditation

While in a state of deep meditation, Sri Chinmoy plays his haunting melodies on the echo flute. Ideal for inspiration in your personal meditation.

CD, $12.95

To Order

Send check or money order made out to Aum Publications. Mail to: Aum Publications, 86-10 Parsons Blvd., Jamaica, NY 11432. Please add $2.50 postage for first book and 50¢ for each additional book.

You have begun your Eternity's journey in Heaven. Now you must continue it here on earth.

We are always apt to say that it is not too late to do anything, but do we ever say that it is not too early to do anything? It is not too early to do anything in life. It is not too early to pray in the small hours of the morning. It is not too early to realise God. It is not too early to reveal God. It is not too early to manifest God. The sooner we realise God, the sooner we reveal God, the sooner we manifest God, the sooner we will start with a new beginning, aiming at a higher, more illumining, more fulfilling goal.

A sincere seeker knows
That his aspiration-life
Is nothing short of
A lifetime opportunity
To realise God
And to become inseparably one
With God's manifestation-light
On earth.

BIOGRAPHICAL NOTE

Sri Chinmoy, was born in East Bengal, India (now Bangladesh), in 1931. When orphaned at the age of 13, he entered the Sri Aurobindo Ashram in south India, where he prayed and meditated for several hours a day, having many deep inner experiences. He also took an active part in ashram life and was decathlete champion for several years. It was here that he first began writing poetry to convey his widening mystical vision.

After coming to the United States in 1964, Sri Chinmoy continued his literary activities—eventually completing thousands of poems, essays and questions and answers, as well as large numbers of paintings, drawings and songs. His poetry touches upon virtually every aspect of the spiritual journey—from the struggles and wonderment of the young pilgrim to the ecstatic realisations of the illumined Master. His prose is equally encompassing—focusing on man's relationship with God, global peace, worlds beyond the mind and the vast universe within. Viewed as a whole, his writings offer a unique, deeply spiritual, luminous world view.

Sri Chinmoy's creative output grew out of his work as a teacher and man of peace. During the years he lived in the West, he opened more than 100 meditation Centres worldwide and served as spiritual guide to multitudes of students. He offered twice-weekly meditations at the United Nations and gave hundreds of peace concerts in the U.S. and overseas. In addition, he founded the World Harmony Run, a biennial Olympic-style relay in which runners pass a flaming peace torch from hand to hand as they travel around the globe. He also promoted international good will through his own athletic endeavors, primarily weightlifting, and towards the end of his life worked tirelessly to encourage peace through sports. Sri Chinmoy died in 2007 at the age of 76.

OTHER BOOKS BY SRI CHINMOY

Grace

Sri Chinmoy describes the constant flow of Grace from Above and explains how we can become more receptive to it. $5.00

Compassion

It is God's Compassion that is moulding us, guiding us and illumining us at every step of our journey through life. In this book Sri Chinmoy teaches us how to recognise, experience it and distribute this Compassion to those around us. $5.00

Forgiveness

Sri Chinmoy offers his illumining guidance on how to seek divine Forgiveness. $5.00

Meditation: Man-Perfection in God-Satisfaction

Presented with the simplicity and clarity that have become the hallmark of Sri Chinmoy's writings, this book is one of the most comprehensive guides to meditation available. $11.95

Beyond Within: A Philosophy for the Inner Life

Sri Chinmoy offers profound insight into humanity's relationship with God, and sound advice on how to integrate the highest spiritual aspirations into daily life. $13.95

My Life's Soul-Journey: Daily Meditations for Ever-Increasing Spiritual Fulfilment

In this volume of daily meditations, each day's offering resonates with the innate goodness of humanity and encourages the reader to bring this goodness to the fore. $13.95

Death and Reincarnation

This deeply moving book has brought consolation and understanding to countless people faced with the loss of a loved one or fear of their own mortality. Sri Chinmoy explains the secrets of death, the afterlife and reincarnation. $7.95

Yoga and the Spiritual Life

Specifically tailored for Western readers, this book offers rare insight into the philosophy of Yoga and Eastern mysticism. $8.95

The Summits of God-Life: Samadhi and Siddhi

A genuine account of the world beyond time and space, this is Sri Chinmoy's first-hand account of states of consciousness that only a handful of Masters have ever experienced. $6.95

The Three Branches of India's Life-Tree: Commentaries on the Vedas, the Upanishads and the Bhagavad Gita

This book is both an excellent introduction for readers who are coming to these Hindu classics for the first time, and a series of illumining meditations for those who already know them well. $13.95

Kundalini: The Mother-Power

Sri Chinmoy explains techniques for awakening the Kundalini and the chakras, warns of the dangers and pitfalls to be avoided, and discusses some of the occult powers that can be developed.
$7.95

The Inner Promise: Sri Chinmoy's University Talks

Speaking in a state of deep meditation during these 42 talks, Sri Chinmoy filled the audience with a serenity many had never before experienced. They found his words, as a faculty member later put it, to be "living seeds of spirituality."
$14.95

Everest-Aspiration

Inspired talks on a wide variety of spiritual themes.
$9.95

A Child's Heart and a Child's Dream: Growing Up with Spiritual Wisdom—A Guide for Parents and Children

Sri Chinmoy offers practical advice on fostering your child's spiritual life, watching him or her grow up with a love of God and a heart of self-giving.
$7.95

The Master and the Disciple

Sri Chinmoy says in this definitive book on the Guru-disciple relationship: "The most important thing a Guru does for his spiritual children is to make them aware of something vast and infinite within themselves, which is nothing other than God Himself."
$7.95

Siddhartha Becomes the Buddha

The combination of profound insight and simplicity of language makes this book an excellent choice for anyone, young or old, seeking to understand one of the world's most influential spiritual figures. $6.95

Music by Sri Chinmoy

Flute Music for Meditation

While in a state of deep meditation, Sri Chinmoy plays his haunting melodies on the echo flute. Ideal for inspiration in your personal meditation.

CD, $12.95

To Order

Send check or money order made out to Aum Publications. Mail to: Aum Publications, 86-10 Parsons Blvd., Jamaica, NY 11432. Please add $2.50 postage for first book and 50¢ for each additional book.